Deedee Divine's

TOTALLY SKEWED GUIDE TO LIFE

Happy Bday
Maggie!
For one who can
appreciate this
sort of lifestyle!
xoo [illegible]

Also by Diana Estill

Driving on the Wrong Side of the Road: Humorous Views on Love, Lust, & Lawn Care

Deedee Divine's
TOTALLY SKEWED GUIDE TO LIFE

DIANA ESTILL

Deedee Divine's Totally Skewed Guide to Life

For information about special discounts for bulk purchases, contact:

Corncob Press c/o
Totally Skewed Productions
120 E. FM 544, Suite 72, PMB 135
Murphy, TX 75094

ISBN-13: 978-0-9799708-1-8

ISBN-10: 0-9799708-1-4

Library of Congress Control Number: 2008908293

1 2 3 4 5 6 7 8 9 10

First Edition

www.TotallySkewed.com

To the memory of

Genevieve "Sis" Kerley

1910 – 2006

Loving grandmother and a friend to all.

CONTENTS

Introduction

Who, exactly, is Deedee Divine? Well, she is me—and you or your sister or maybe your friend. Because when you get right down to it, everyone has multiple personalities. From the reserved and confident side we exhibit in our professional lives to the wild-eyed screaming banshee selves we unleash only on our closest kin, every facet of our being demands its day. Different environments simply call for different degrees of self-restraint. That's precisely why Deedee Divine was born.

At times I find it difficult to behave like the uncensored, quirky, and irreverent gal I can be when surrounded by my most forgiving pals. That's when I simply get out of the way and let Deedee take over. Deedee is the part of me that doesn't hold back, the woman who voices strong and totally skewed views for which she offers no apologies.

In her younger years, Deedee was much less vocal. But now, with more than a half century of experiences behind her, she no longer looks at life from a bubble-on-due-plumb perspective. Laughter is what's gotten her through the hard patches, plummeting times, and spiraling bills. That's why she feels it's important to help others find the fun in their frustrations, to locate the levity that exists everywhere from the roadways to the kitchen. A Southwestern woman of modest intelligence and bold opinions, she suggests there's always more than one method for greasing a pig—and a variety of ways to barbecue that oinker.

In this book you'll discover how Deedee manages everything from her weight (following "Deedee's Flavorless Diet" and working out with a mattress cover) to her husband and household (ignoring both when that's convenient). She'll examine myths, such as the existence of long-term romance, and proffer advice on parenting daredevil children and keeping the holidays "lite" without resorting to imitation beer.

I hope you enjoy reading *Deedee Divine's Totally Skewed Guide to Life*. If you'd like to give Deedee a shout or offer your own tidbits for handling turmoil, please drop me a line and I'll be sure to see that Deedee gets your message.

Diana
(aka/Deedee)

Diana

www.TotallySkewed.com

FAMILY THAT
DOESN'T KILL YOU
MAKES YOU STRONGER

Licking Motherhood

There are days when I question my capabilities as a mom. Did I get it right when I was raising my four children? Even once? Like the late humorist Erma Bombeck said, "Who knows? I showed up."

What, exactly, are the roles of a mother? Some of them are repeated so often that we can recite them like the Pledge of Allegiance: feed, clothe, nurture, and nag. But there are others less easily recognized. For instance, I am absolutely the only person on the planet who can, when my grown son asks, definitively state the hour of his birth. Mothers can do this. Fathers, on the other hand, seldom remember. That could be because they weren't the ones doing all of the pushing.

We moms are the ones who wreck our bodies, wear out our vocal chords, and ruin our vehicles for the sole benefit of offspring who will not give any of our selfless acts a second thought until they, themselves, become parents. It's rewarding to observe those rebellious young-ones-turned-adults revisiting upon their children some of the very acts—using spit to perform emergency facial cleansings, squeezing someone else's zit—they previously found so repulsive. These are among a mother's sacrificial duties.

We feed our children potted meats and Spam, and are kind enough never to tell them what ingredients these foods contain. And we spare our little ones the truth about the link between Easter pets and chicken nuggets.

Mothers have a keen sense of smell combined with superior reasoning skills. God gave us these abilities for a purpose. We're the first to know when it's time to change a diaper and yet cunning enough to convince Dad to do the job.

As family historians, we're the keepers of our kiddos' nightmares, proof of their dependent origins, and preservationists of all that our progeny would just as soon forget. We are the repository of prime information, such as developmental milestones, pathetic prom dates, and imperfect driving records.

We hang onto old photos depicting mullet hairstyles, dresses with football uniform-like shoulder pads, and Sally Jessie-Raphael-inspired eyewear, knowing fully well that one day these pictures will entertain our children's future spouses. None of this is malicious. It's just our way of making sure we don't raise narcissists.

How do we ever know if we've done all that's been expected of us as mothers? We do the best we can. Then if one day we observe one of our offspring taking a tongue-moistened finger to his or her child's face, it's a positive sign.

Too Much Information May Cause Death

In the event of my unexplained demise, please interview my family for clues. They'll be the first to tell you that I harbor the common, though potentially fatal, WAE (worry about everything) gene, a condition I inherited from my paternal grandmother.

Whenever my father traveled on vacation, Grandma would call me within minutes of his departure. "Do you have any word of his whereabouts?" she'd ask. And then I'd tell her that he was currently backing out of his driveway.

By the third day, her pleas for information would arrive replete with stories of breaking news occurring on the opposite coast from wherever Dad might have been. And within less than a week, Grandma would be begging to know if anyone had yet found "the body."

This genetically acquired affliction causes me to suffer bouts of nausea, pain, and abnormal sleep positions any time my loved ones undertake extreme risks. These hazards include embarking upon trips to dangerous places like Mexico, Europe, and Best Buy. Hence, my kinfolks have to exercise caution about what information they reveal.

"I'm home from the hospital," my mother chirped over the telephone. She works two days a week as a health care volunteer, so this was a fairly regular report until she added, "You know, I've been in there since Tuesday—with pneumonia."

"What?" I cried. "You were in the hospital and didn't tell me?"

"Well," Mom confessed, laughing, "I didn't want you to worry."

Later that day, my daughter, who suffers chronic knee problems, arrived for a visit. She chatted for a while and then, as she was leaving, offered, "Oh, I almost forgot to tell you. I'm going skiing for a few days."

"Skiing?" I echoed. "You don't know how to ski. You'll break a leg!"

"See. That's exactly why I wasn't going to tell you," she replied, dismissing my concerns.

"You can't go skiing now," I said. "How am I going to visit you in a Colorado hospital if I'm taking care of Mom in Florida?"

"I'm not going to be in a hospital," she stressed. "I'm going to be with my boyfriend."

"Boyfriend?" I yelped. "Not the guy you said you dumped three months ago?"

She was out the door and gone before I could elicit any details.

Frustrated, I retreated to my office and logged on to the Internet. That's when I encountered an e-mail message from my son that said, "Mom, please take a look at this and tell me what you think." Opening the attachment, I found his letter of application—to a police bomb squad.

Doctors here say that my prognosis remains good. But if I should keel over, someone should investigate the family for collusion.

Daredevil Children

It's not unusual for a mother to have a daredevil child, one youngster whose sole objective appears to be to make his or her parents nervous. For some reason, I was blessed with two.

The eldest became a police officer. The second turned out to be a competitive risk taker. In her most recent attempt to outdo a friend, she jumped from an airplane flying at 13,500 feet—on purpose.

I've no idea where these kids acquired their fearlessness. It certainly wasn't from me. I won't even get within 1,000 feet of a roller coaster—much less ride one. But two of my adult children would declare the space shuttle a kiddie ride.

As you might expect, I spend a great deal of time worrying.

"Tell me again why you're doing this," I probed when my daughter Laura called to announce she'd decided to skydive.

"I think it'll be fun," she said brightly. "One of my friends has done it before, and I saw her video."

Mentally, I made a note to never have the Discovery Channel on when Laura is visiting.

"When are you doing this?" I asked. Maybe there was still time to talk her down.

"At three," she replied.

"Today?"

Laura gave out a laugh that suggested "gotcha." Then she paused. "It'll be okay. I'm getting a little nervous, though. There's a part of me that's saying, 'Don't do this.'"

"That's the self-preservation part that's speaking to you right now," I said. "And maybe you ought to be listening."

Though I gave it my best shot, explained how difficult it would be to Salsa dance with two broken ankles, suggested that a belly-flop on a rooftop might hurt a great deal more than one suffered in a swimming pool, I couldn't persuade her to cancel the jump.

"Where are you supposed to land?" I asked, realizing I had better learn the particulars.

Through the phone line, I heard what sounded like keystrokes. "I'm looking that up right now," Laura said in her most professional voice.

"You don't even know where you're *supposed* to land?" I beseeched.

"Here it is, right here," she said. "Someplace called Whitewright. The dirt is supposed to be really soft there."

I clung to the handset, realizing this could be our last conversation. Why, why, why did this child have to be so adventuresome? Hadn't I taught her anything during all those years of travel mishaps and fun avoidance?

"I'm not eating anything before I jump," she said. "I saw this video of one woman who made that mistake, and when she landed ... well, let's just say she had to change her underwear."

To me, this sounded like a perfectly legitimate response to a free fall from a few miles above the earth.

Her tone now more serious, she offered, "That would

be my greatest fear. A real MasterCard moment, don't you know?" She chuckled. "Parachuting from plane: $250. Video of me crapping my pants: priceless."

Wonderful, I thought. She's not afraid to die, but she's afraid of having poopy drawers.

"I'll call you when I hit the ground," she said. "Well, not 'hit the ground.' You know, land."

Later that evening, according to my telephone caller ID, Laura finally did attempt to contact me, but she didn't leave a message. I'm sure she meant to. Right then, another death-defying opportunity probably arose. Maybe a friend broke out a motocross video or an Amazon River trip brochure, and Laura got sidetracked. Already, I'm sure she's planning her next excursion.

It's obviously too late for me. The damage has been done. However, for anyone who's currently toilet training children, be extremely cautious. If you're not careful, things can go haywire. And then you'll end up with grown children like mine, offspring who fear only the wrong kinds of accidents.

What's DNA Got to Do with It?

What makes a child *your* child? Certainly it's not the physical act of giving birth. Too many individuals are raising non-biological broods for this to be the case. However, childbirth does provide some advantages, such as valid excuses for weight gain, drooping flesh, and unsightly stretch pants.

Having acquired two of my four children through a midlife marriage and a blended household, I've decided a youngster becomes yours when you care enough to say, "Don't do that. You're going to hurt yourself." This is especially true if you also happen to be responsible for paying his or her medical bills.

"I'm going skiing," my 28-year-old daughter, Laura, enthused. Though she's only been in my life since age 12, I knew she lacked any prior exposure to hazards like ski lifts, killer trees, and sports instructors. Carefully, I relayed to her the outcome of my one and only encounter with a pair of snow skis.

I never was coordinated enough to ski beyond the bunny slopes. Whenever I tried to tackle the mountains, they pretty much beat me stupid, which could explain my sense of humor. How I feel about this sport can best be summarized this way:

The effects of skiing are a lot like being in multiple car wrecks within the same day, yet considerably more bruising.

After first describing how I had to take ski lessons, twice, just to master the art of standing without supports (ski poles), I detailed the numerous ways people can make idiots of themselves while dismounting from a ski lift. "You have to jump off at the exact moment you're supposed to," I explained. "Otherwise, the bench starts back down the mountain. Not only does this annoy the heck out of the lift operator, but it can be maddening to your ski partner."

Laura snickered. "If I can jump out of an airplane, I can probably handle a ski lift," she mused.

My skydiving gal was right. Once again, I had to remind myself that though I'd helped usher her through puberty, she did not share my DNA. Perhaps she'd been lucky enough to escape the gene responsible for making me an athletic klutz.

On the second day of her winter vacation, Laura called me.

"Where are you?" I asked.

"I'm inside the lodge," she replied, her voice unnaturally flat. Then she blurted, "Omigod, Mom, I've never been so scared in my whole life!"

"What happened?" I cried. I envisioned her sitting there in a wheelchair, both legs in casts that stretched from her arches to her thighs.

"I got up there on that mountain, and I realized how straight down it was, and there was no way out but to ski." She groaned. "I mean there wasn't an elevator or anything. And I didn't want to do this, so I started crying—and my boyfriend took off and left me standing there!"

From the sound of her voice I could tell she'd been mentally shaken. Not only was she unwilling to ski any more for the remainder of the day but, quite possibly, for the rest of her life.

"I can't wait to get back home where it's warm," she declared. "Next time, I'm going to take a tropical vacation where you just sit on the beach in the sand."

After I assured her there would be life after humiliation, we ended our conversation. Briefly I chuckled over the image she'd described. She'd evidently become entangled in her skis and fallen from the lift chair. "And those darn things don't stop when that happens!" she stressed, as if I might not have had a clear picture of what followed.

All I could think was, "Yep, she's my daughter."

Child Safety Seat Emergency

When I learned I'd be the stand-in chauffeur for my grandson Heath, I nearly hyperventilated.

"You'll need to write his name on a big sheet of paper with a marker," my daughter-in-law advised. "Hold it up where they can see it when you're approaching."

I'd never had to follow such a procedure for my own children. But then again, my kids hadn't attended preschool at age 2.

It wasn't the driving or delivery that worried me, but rather the thought of maneuvering a child safety seat. Anyone who's ever wrestled with a child's safety seat knows that some of these contraptions require an engineering degree to install.

By telephone, Heath's mother provided me instructions. "It's sort of like a puzzle." She gave a nervous laugh. "You have to pull the harness part down over his head, of course. And then you grab the two metal pieces from either side and overlap them—I think it's the left one over the right one—or maybe it's the other way around. It's kind of tricky," she said.

I could envision the outcome perfectly, a breaking news piece: *This just in ... Woman and child stranded in church school parking lot for hours after grandmother unable to secure child's car seat.* Overhead a few helicopters would circle, filming, while do-gooders dispensed the victim bottled juice and animal crackers. I would be the lady off in the shadows, cowering before police and child protection workers.

As my departure time drew near, I could feel my pulse pounding like the theme music from 24. This stress, of course, caused me to obsess about food. And then it dawned on me: I could use treats to keep my passenger happy.

Armed with a stick of string cheese, a bag of raisins, and a juice box, I embarked on my journey—accidentally leaving behind my handwritten directions to the church.

God must watch out for little children because when I couldn't recollect which way to go, I whipped into a parking lot to my right and realized I'd turned directly into the church school lineup.

A teacher walked my grandson to the car and offered to situate the safety seat, which further evidenced divine intervention. Heath chatted and ate his raisins while I thanked my Maker for saving the day.

Back at my house, though, this experience abruptly changed.

I had to get Heath *out* of his restraining device, so I pushed the red button and tried to lift the bar over his head. Quickly I registered that he looked like a hold-up victim. Somehow his arms were still locked into his car seat. I lowered the safety lever and tried again, so now he appeared to be doing The Wave.

Feeling over and under the mechanism, I couldn't find any other release clasps. Frantically, I tugged and pulled on each of the harness sections to no avail. Heath studied me intently, his expression one of impatience. After several minutes, I considered whether my next call should be directed to the local fire department.

"I'm sorry, Sweetie," I said. "I can't figure out how to unlatch this thing."

Heath screwed up his face and looked as if he might let out a wail. But instead he reached out one arm, crossed his chest and pointed to a black circular indentation in the middle of the harness.

"Here," he said.

I pushed where he'd indicated, and the harness straps released.

In case of a safety seat emergency, always remember to seek guidance from the expert. This will save you from embarrassing phone calls and shameful news headlines.

Father Knows Frugal

From personal experience, I can tell you that women are the experts when it comes to spending with wild, dare I say primal, abandon. We are gatherers, collectors of all things advertised and sold exclusively through mass merchandisers and home shopping channels. Men, especially ones like my dad, do not know how to seriously splurge—except when they're inside a building materials or consumer electronics store.

To be truthful, which isn't nearly as much fun as telling a fib, my father has never indulged in anything except vacations and construction projects. Dad can't tell you the difference between Tiffany & Co. and Timex. But he can discuss, ad infinitum, various grades of lumber, drywall, and his favorite artistic medium: concrete.

Growing up with a father like mine wasn't easy. When I was a teenager, Dad deprived me of critical products like Bobbie Brooks sportswear and Herbal Essences shampoo. In place of these, he forced me to substitute low-priced discount store jeans and cheap hair care products. And though this might have saved a fair amount of money, it led directly to me being ostracized, and ultimately rejected, by "the popular crowd."

As head of household, my father demanded that the family be satisfied with generic brand items. Mom was permitted to purchase canned goods only if they carried product names like Bland Brand Beans and Mystery Meat Mush. We drank colas that couldn't be identified and frequented the "day-old" grocers' racks, hoping to find hidden Hostess treasures.

I hated shopping with Dad.

"If we hurry, I bet we can make it home before this turns green," my frugal father would say. "There's at least a half-hour remaining on the expiration date."

So I learned a few important lessons early in life: Man cannot live by stale bread alone, and freshness is next to godliness.

Not much has changed through the years. My father still shops exclusively from discounters and home improvement stores. And despite living in the 'burbs, he grows vegetables (tomatoes and six-foot tall okra plants) in his flower beds.

Though never fun, it used to be easy to buy Dad a gift. All I had to do was get him a new set of drill bits, a laser stud-finder (Where were these things when I was younger?), or a quality power tool of some sort, and he'd be happy. But now that he's past 70 years of age, I hate to encourage such industrious behaviors. Perhaps I should help him focus on more age-appropriate pursuits—like loaning me money.

I could always buy him another book about World War II, the war he never fought in but can't seem to learn enough about. He'd also enjoy any CD made by a dead country artist. You might say he's still enamored with expiration dates.

Maybe I should get Dad a pair of those binoculars that can snap digital photos. The best ones cost about $350. However, on the Internet I found a set made by Cop-a-View value priced at just $34.95. These are bound to work as well as the more expensive versions, right?

I think I'll save the cash and buy the cheaper set. Surely a guy like my dad would appreciate that.

No Happy July 4 Campers

Over time and with repetition, certain summer activities can lose their luster. Case in point: camping. Don't ask me to pitch a tent. I'd rather go run with the bulls in Pamplona, a Spanish extreme sport in which participants permit stampeding bovine to chase them for no apparent reason.

Camping too is a dangerous activity. Think about it. You're out there in the wilderness with the snakes, bears, and mountain lions, sleeping near people (possibly recent parolees) who are armed with poles, axes, and unlimited beer.

When my youngest was still willing to be seen with me, our family camped our way across America in pup tents, fabric shelters named for the size animal they can comfortably house. Some folks call a pup tent a two-man tent, but that's misleading. Two men would have to be extraordinarily close to share such cramped sleeping quarters.

The tent that my husband and I slept in fit neatly inside a travel tote. At least, it did the day we purchased it. However, every time we tried to break down a campsite, the billowy contraption refused to return to its original size. So, we developed this formula for stowing away a tent:

1. Spread the flattened tent out on the ground or pavement.

2. Make sure all the stakes have been removed.

3. Crease the nylon material into smaller and smaller folds until you have a bundle no larger than a couch.

4. Back your vehicle over the tent several times, and then fold again.

One Fourth of July weekend, my husband Jim, oldest son Ron, his wife, and my youngest boy and I decided to pitch camp at Possum Kingdom State Park. This taught me a few important lessons. First, July 4 is not the most opportune time to sleep outdoors. And second, when the external temperature is 98 degrees at midnight, two bodies crammed inside a nylon tent could be cause for murder.

"I can't take another minute of this heat," I snapped. "Get your arm off of me."

"Where would you like me to put it?" Jim asked.

"How about in the nearest Best Western? And take me with it."

He pushed the backlight button on his watch. "It's 1:15 in the morning on a holiday weekend. You're not being reasonable."

On the verge of spontaneous combustion, I stormed out of the tent and headed for open air. Ron met me as he was exiting from his own dome-shaped sauna. "Good gr-r-ief!"

he shouted. "I've got to find a breeze before I *die*!"

Five minutes later, everyone was up and scrambling for the ice chest.

Finally, after a 20-minute family gripe session, we parted company in search of new places to sweat out the night. Jim and Ron claimed the front seats of our car, cranked the engine and turned the air conditioner setting to permafrost. Realizing this was not a practical arrangement, I settled atop our picnic table. The others had already wisely bedded down in the back of Ron's pickup truck.

I'd almost dozed off when I heard something stirring underneath me. "There's something out here," I called to anyone within hearing range.

More scratches and scuffles, followed by paper crunching.

"Y'all! There's something under this table. Will somebody shine a light over here?" I begged.

From the sedan's now open driver-side door, Ron lobbed a rock towards me. "That ought to scare off whatever it is," he said.

Grrrrr-rrrrrr, responded an angry animal.

"It's somebody's dog," I cried. "One of you had better get out here and get this thing away from me right now!"

Someone aimed a flashlight my direction.

"It's not a dog," Jim dryly remarked.

I peered over the edge of my makeshift mattress and right into the eyes of a horribly annoyed skunk.

That put an end to my tent camping.

Welcome to Camp Grandma

My childhood summers included cross-country camping trips during which our six-member family forgot all about bonding, contented instead with mere survival.

I spent most of this time begrudgingly staring at historical markers and praying for severe weather. Violent thunderstorms were the only threats capable of making Dad shell out the funds for a motel stay. Why pay to sleep in a bed, he reasoned, when we had a perfectly good tent and some swim mattresses?

Needless to say, children's camps were never part of my seasonal experience. Dad probably thought expensive summer camps were for kids who didn't have adventuresome parents or healthy grandmas.

Every summer, my grandmother invited my cousin and me to stay with her for a week. You might say this was my first exposure to a bed-and-breakfast: old farmhouse, iron bed, and home-cooked meals prepared by a woman who never received a break.

Grandma showered us with love and attention. When she wasn't looking, we repaid her by getting into everything she'd ever told us was off limits.

I explored my grandmother's perfumes and cold creams, examined her jewelry, and searched through dresser drawers for hidden treasures. My cousin followed suit by emptying bookshelves, inventorying the fridge, and tinkering with bathroom toiletries.

Now that I'm a grandma, myself, I realize that children need rules when visiting relatives, written rules posted someplace they'll frequent—like maybe the refrigerator or, in my case, the attic door. That's why I've developed the following directives for what I've dubbed "Camp Grandma":

Meals

Breakfasts will be served until 10:00 a.m., and, depending on the hour of request, will consist of hot items, cold cereal, or lukewarm fruit rollups.

Lunches may be provided off-premise, but in no event shall chicken nuggets be consumed more than once per day.

Dinners will be confined to entrees from the camp's pantry, refrigerator, or freezer—or from the restaurant of choice anytime campers are prepared to pay the bill.

Activities

Finger painting is allowed. Furniture painting is not.

Drawing is encouraged, so long as campers are not penciling body tattoos with a permanent marker.

When swimming, campers must be accompanied by an adult at all times. Grandma will not enter the pool when water temperatures are below 80 degrees or anyone else is around to witness her in a swimsuit.

Movie outings may be offered. Grandma reserves the right to refuse excessive requests for popcorn, sodas, candies, video games, and other overpriced and cruelly marketed items.

Housekeeping

The sofa is for sitting or reclining, not vaulting.

Telephones may be used to call your parents but not to text the Jonas Brothers or Hannah Montana.

Showers are mandatory. This should not prompt the need for flood insurance.

Bedtimes shall be established arbitrarily by Grandma, based solely on her energy levels.

When departing, be sure to leave with everything you arrived with, including your parents.

Perhaps these rules seem a bit rigid but, hey, it could be worse. My grandchildren could be standing in the searing heat in the middle of nowhere, staring blankly at a historical marker for something that's no longer even there.

How to Organize a Family Gathering

As it stands right now, at my house we'll be celebrating Thanksgiving in February and Christmas in March. I envy those whose family gatherings coincide with the traditional calendar, but my bunch refuses to cooperate. To get all my relatives collected in the same place at once requires a GPS, special software, and a direct offer of free cash.

"I won't be in town on your birthday," my father said. "We're going to be traveling. Can we get everyone together for dinner sometime the following weekend?"

"I'll check and get back to you," I replied, knowing fully well what this meant.

Being the social coordinator for my family is like managing media relations for Britney Spears. I can't help questioning whether the required spin justifies the final outcome.

Dad spends more time away from home than a corporate outsourcing consultant. My son's work schedule shifts as abruptly as the Dow Jones Industrial Average. And book promotions keep me Tangoing across Texas to stay ahead of expenses.

"What hours are you working this month?" I asked my son.

"I don't have any weekends off," he said. "How about next month?"

"Next month are Jim's and your grandmother's birthdays," I reminded him.

"Oh, yeah," he acknowledged. "Maybe we should do one big get-together for all three of you."

Sure, I thought. This way, I'd need to corral my free-roaming kin for only one event.

First, I called my daughter-in-law, who reviewed my granddaughter's soccer schedule. She read off a litany of games so fast that I didn't have time to write them all down. Only one Saturday held any potential.

Confounded, I scratched out calendar dates. "Let me call you back," I said.

Surely my daughter, who's single and has no children, would be easier to corner. "What Saturdays are you free within the next two months?" I asked by phone.

"Oh, my boss says since we're so far behind with our work, everyone is going to have to start working Saturdays." She sighed. "Maybe we'll be caught up by December. Can we do it then?"

"Gee, I kind of thought we'd be having our holiday dinner that month," I offered. "But I guess we could push Christmas out until January."

I informed my spouse that, to make way for all the belated birthday celebrations, we'd be honoring the arrival of Jesus in January. "Nobody knows for sure when He was born, anyway," I rationalized. "It might have been February, March, or even April."

"Good," said hubby, "because January is a busy month for me. Can we do it later in the year?"

"Wait a minute," I whined, fumbling with my computer. "I

can't possibly handle all this without opening a spreadsheet."

"When are we doing Thanksgiving?" he fired back. "What day have you booked for that?"

"What do you expect from me?" I snapped. My fingers trembled as I hammered on the keyboard. "For crying out loud, can't you see I'm still working on the September and October birthdays? I'm not a professional event planner! Give me a break."

I've since downloaded project management software, the kind used by astronomers to predict the probability of interstellar debris colliding with Planet Earth. According to my new sophisticated system, our next chance to have a family dinner will occur in February—right after I announce that the will is being revised.

FOOD & FITNESS
(LOST IN TASTE)

Juicing January

I dislike January for one simple reason; it's a time of reckoning, a period when I must admit I failed to lose the weight I promised to shed 12 months earlier. And worse, those sinister pounds left over from the prior year have not only persisted, but like a bunch of amoebas, they've divided and multiplied. So now instead of simply needing to lose a few kilos, I've become a candidate for a new television feature: *Fat Columnist*.

Like many this time of year, I'm obsessed with the idea, if not the actual production, of weight loss. And the first place I turn when I'm starving for information (instead of for enchiladas and guacamole) is my local bookstore. As soon as I've downed a few scones in the store's coffee house, I head for the diet and health section, where I peruse the latest fad diets and workout regimens to see what I might use for my next excuse.

My husband has adopted this behavior, too. We both follow the same pattern: display mock concern over weight gain, research the latest nutrition news and workout gadgets, and then finally blame our prior failures on lack of proper a.) knowledge, b.) equipment, and c.) supplements only movie stars can afford. Then we revert back to our normal eating and exercise routines.

Standing in the bookstore aisle, I couldn't help marveling at the plethora of diet programs that currently exist. I mean, how many ways can you say, "Eat less, exercise more?" Apparently, quite a few. For me, here's where the difficulties arise; I'm already eating less than most—less produce, and definitely less variety—and I'm still not slender!

One diet book author states that he consumes his vegetables juiced. Well, if I were juiced, I'd probably eat Bermuda grass. But I think he meant the vegetables were liquefied.

Instantly, my partner latched onto this. "I might have eaten more raw vegetables and lost more weight if we'd had a *juicer,*" he declared.

"What's the difference between a juicer and a blender?" I scoffed. "Besides, you could have shoved a cucumber and some cabbage into our food processor and achieved the same results."

"No. It says right here," he insisted, pointing to one paragraph. "They're not the same."

Now, I don't understand the need for a juicer. We could have used the money my husband spent on that gadget to purchase something we'd actually enjoy, like, say, a chocolate fondue set.

Nonetheless, he had to prove his point, which was that he would use this countertop consuming contraption. After he spent hours racking up a three-figure grocery bill, my newly health-conscious mate came home with a stash of collard greens, cabbage, cucumbers, bell peppers, lettuce, broccoli, and something that could double for dandelion weeds. I couldn't wait to see him drink that concoction! This alone would justify the price of the juicer.

When he poured the green sludge into his glass, I looked

on with astonishment. It was sort of like watching one of those gross eating contests, only better. This guy was standing right in front of me, about to chug-a-lug a tumbler full of pond algae. That drink couldn't have appeared less enticing if I'd emptied it straight from the kitchen food disposal, but he was too far into this adventure to turn back.

He downed a thick gulp and gagged.

Now we have a head start on our excuses for next year. My hubby might have lost more weight if he could have drunk his vegetables. And watching this would have generated sufficient nausea to melt me into a size 6. Thankfully, I can say with confidence that the pressure is now off.

Eaters Can be Cheaters

My husband was called out of town on business for several days, which triggered me to behave like some wild, carefree bachelorette. Before I'd even realized the transformation occurring, I found myself inside a place where I was seriously at risk. I had no business being there, and I knew it. With my husband gone, there was no cause for me to visit the grocery store.

Normally, I have to be accountable for the foods I buy and store in my pantry and fridge. But for the next four glorious days, this would not be the case. I could eat anything ... ANYTHING. The options suddenly seemed deliciously tempting and overwhelmingly available. Aisles and shelves of delectable items: corn chips, squirt cheese, mixed nuts, chocolate candies, and cookies begged me to sample their comforts. These snack items, I knew, had long been attracted to my thighs. I heard one of them whistle when I passed by.

In my mind, I felt entitled to a fling. After all, my mate would be in New York City dining in SoHo or Little Italy, immersed in culture and real cannoli (not the fake kind we're served here in Texas), while I was home struggling to manage six separate remote controllers. He'd never know what sordid combination of goodies I'd purchased or ingested while he was away. By the time he returned, I would have destroyed all evidence of my wandering appetite.

With a firm grip and equally firm resolve, I wheeled my buggy into action. Right off, the Flamin' Hot Cheetos appealed to my desire for something naughty and saucy. But the butter-flavored kettle corn promised greater "pop per penny." Who says I can't have a little *ménage à trois*? Am I not woman enough to handle both? I tossed these temptations into my cart and continued on.

Then I saw it, right there on the same aisle, the tin of honey-roasted nuts that guaranteed a sexy aroma. Did I want the 7-ounce can or the lap-band-surgery-here-I-come-size container? If I didn't get too greedy, I might still have room for the double-crust pizza and peanut butter-filled Oreo cookies I'd been craving.

You could argue that, after all this, I didn't need those two king-size dark chocolate bars. However, to do so would be to overlook the digestive health benefits of cocoa and its sheer animal-like attraction. Rich, creamy, chocolate, with its handsome smoothness and alluring flavor, as anyone knows, is irresistible. Sure, I could have just said no, but why would I have wanted to?

Moments later, I glimpsed the store's magazine rack. If I'd had a mirror to check, I'm pretty sure I'd have witnessed my pupils dilate. The lyrics to "Some Enchanted Evening" echoed in my mind, providing a soundtrack for my fantasies. Knees trembling, pulse quickening, I sashayed over to the eye candy and shamelessly cruised for content.

It started out rather harmlessly with a copy of *Woman's Day* that offered 235 gift ideas and recipes with no more than seven ingredients. But then my addiction for information turned to *The Old Farmer's Almanac,* a publication to help me discuss important topics like the weather. After that, I spotted a travel magazine that displayed a shirtless hunk wearing swim trunks and standing on a white powdery beach. I'd like to say I showed some restraint. But I didn't. I took all three as evening companions.

When my spouse returned home, he suspected I'd been up to no good. Though I'd removed the candy wrappers from the nightstand and cleaned the cookie crumbs off the kitchen counter, the bedding provided incriminating evidence. I couldn't explain the stains, so I had to confess. Obviously, I'd cheated with a pizza.

Oh, Woe Is March

Though often overlooked by those who lack a spring break, March is a significant month. Fully one-twelfth of all calendar days occur within this period. But aside from that, March also has been designated Irish-American History Month, Women's History Month, and Optimist Month. So if you know any optimistic Irish women (this could be an oxymoron), then please be sure to celebrate them.

In addition to St. Patrick's Day, spring officially arrives in March, and so do those Girl Scout cookies that wreck my weight-loss plans. Those shortbread wafers should have been more appropriately named Diet Foils. And let me assure you, there's nothing skinny about Thin Mints.

Spring is a hazardous time for me. Aside from dodging Girl Scouts, it seems that everywhere I turn someone is asking me to either suffer my own pain or subsidize their self-inflicted abuse. Yes, I'm referring to the grueling act of walking.

Now, I realize that this whole charity walk notion has raised a lot of awareness for good causes and sports injury practitioners—but I still question the concept. I mean, I don't get why anyone would expect me to take my normally sedentary self out to some remote mass collection point, from where I'll feel obligated to stroll, limp, or crawl the same distance as all the athletes who've trained and conditioned themselves for years to endure prolonged running escapes from what appears to be an entirely invisible threat. And the winners at these events don't even receive prizes ... because everyone is considered a winner. Where's the fun in that?

Oh, sure, you're going to tell me about the free bottled water, snack bars, and T-shirts that are generously dispensed at these gatherings. But if you ask me, I'd just as soon see the companies who provided these incentives pony up money instead. And I'd prefer to simply write out a donation check without feeling responsible for someone else's agony—especially since I won't be there to see it.

Speaking of pain, during March at my house, we're normally in the throws of tax preparation. I'm telling you, this is more excruciating than being forced to look at Donald Trump's hair. By the time we pay our taxes, everything will be green ... except the insides of our wallets. It's enough to make me want to gorge on another box of those Thin Mints.

Do the Girl Scouts have an emergency hot line?

Deedee's Foolproof Diet

Weight-loss gurus often tout impractical and absurd diets. They push their products and posit their heft-reducing theories, each claiming to have unlocked some previously undiscovered or undisclosed secrets. These hucksters market all kinds of nutrition plans, from the never-eat-anything-bigger-than-your-fist to the fill-up-with-enough-fiber-to-start-your-own-gas-transmission-plant variety.

One man I know, whose name I won't mention, has been following a high-fiber diet so long that he's become a hazard to others' health. In fact, he should be forced to wear a sign that reads: WARNING: CONTENTS UNDER PRESSURE.

The sheer magnitude of weight-loss programs today causes me to develop apathy toward the entire industry. Why would I want to join some fat-reducing organization from the West Coast when I live in Texas? Who wants to spend time counting points or calories? And what's so great about drinking unsweetened green tea? This is the Southwest (home of sweet tea)—not the Orient.

If I have to purchase prepackaged foods sold only through authorized distributors to banish my bulge, then I'll keep my fleshy rolls, thank you very much (and my yeast ones, too). So stop asking. No, I haven't called Jenny!

I prefer to follow a healthy eating program that includes all my food groups: chocolate, ice cream, pizza, fried potatoes, and specialty breads. And finally somebody has developed one; it's called The Flavor Point Diet.

Now, if I correctly understand the concept, The Flavor Point Diet works by flooding your taste buds with one central flavor for an entire day. So on tomato day, for instance, the diet recommends eating tomato products at every meal. The next day, you're instructed to switch to a different flavor, like pineapple.

On tomato day, then, I would eat cold pizza for breakfast, tomato soup with a grilled cheese sandwich on tomato/rosemary bread for lunch, and lasagna for dinner. Somehow I don't see myself shedding much weight on a plan like that. But from a foods permitted standpoint, this program sounds great!

Dr. David Katz, M.D., the author endorsing The Flavor Point Diet, claims that the more you eat of any flavor, the less palatable it becomes. According to that theory, you'll want to consume less of any food once you've reached "sensory-specific satiety." I'm not sure, but I bet this guy's research studies didn't include unlimited servings of potato chips.

After reading about The Flavor Point Diet, I've come up with a foolproof weight-loss program of my own. I call it The Flavorless Diet. Here's how it works:

Allow yourself to eat only bland foods at every meal. Appropriate dishes include plain, unsweetened yogurt, boiled oatmeal without added sweeteners, salad greens with no dressing, celery (no dips), plain chickpeas, and tasteless vegetables such as hominy.

If you're uncertain whether a specific item might be

appropriate for this diet, here's a simple test to help you find out:

1. Take a bite of the food in question.

2. Swirl the sample in your mouth.

3. Determine if this morsel tastes good. Depending on results, follow "a" or "b" below:

    a. If this food holds no appeal, swallow and continue eating.

    b. If you'd like a second sample, spit out the contents. This is not suitable fare for the The Flavorless Diet plan.

Follow this diet for one week, and I guarantee you will have no desire overeat. You'll feel no craving whatsoever to excessively consume any of these foods. And you will absolutely lose weight the whole time you stay on this program, even if you don't exercise.

There's only one drawback; dieters following The Flavorless Diet are advised to wear a sign. To be safe, you'll want to warn those nearby to exercise caution when lighting a flame.

You Snooze, You Lose

Could an extra hour or two of sleep be just as beneficial for your health as exercise? That's what the findings from an *American Journal of Epidemiology* study suggest. Unfortunately, if I want to lose enough pounds to achieve an ideal body weight, I'll have to snooze for a long time—like, say, maybe until my mattress disintegrates.

According to the study results, women who get fewer than seven hours of shuteye per night are more likely to gain weight in midlife than those who catch additional winks. Female participants who slept only five hours per night gained at least 33 pounds more over the course of the 16-year study.

This confirms what I've always suspected: Men ought to leave us gals alone and let us get some rest!

I decided maybe these findings explain why some women, though certainly not any in my family, never gain weight regardless of what they eat.

Here's what I'm going to do the next time I'm out and I see one of those scrawny, size-2 waifs. I'm going to race right up to her, lean in close, and yell, "WAKE UP!"

Okay, you're probably thinking that I'm jealous of adult ladies who can shop in the junior departments. But that's not it. I have nothing against being thin. In fact, I'd probably be a single-digit size myself if I didn't have such a major problem with chronic hunger.

Apparently, I'm not alone. Nearly 70 percent of the U.S. population is now considered overweight or obese (depending on whether you ask them or someone else). The rest of us, I guess, are either movie stars, in rehab, or both.

Folks, this is a crisis!

It's time to declare a National Nap Day. Maybe we could name Al Gore as our Sleep Czar. I know he's a bit preoccupied with global warming right now. But all this extra flab we're carrying (including his) is further heating up our planet!

Something must be done to save our blubbery lot because obesity can lead to hypertension, Type 2 diabetes, and, quite possibly, online dating. If help doesn't arrive soon, virtual romance could become the only kind anyone is capable of having.

Even many of today's toddlers are enormously hefty. I read a recent advertisement for a child safety seat that said the device was suitable "for children 30 to 100 pounds." One hundred pounds? I wasn't that heavy in high school!

A recent study found that the number of children requiring surgery to reduce their obesity has tripled. Researchers expect 1,000 kids to need the surgery within the next 12 months.

But most of the focus seems to be on individual BMI (body mass index) rather than actual load. And this is where I get confused. BMI is based on an individual's height and weight. Since I'm shrinking as I age, it stands to reason that my BMI will automatically increase even if I don't gain another ounce.

I went to ObesityinAmerica.org and used its BMI

calculator to prove this point. At 5' 4", the height I used to be, my BMI is on the cusp between normal and overweight. After losing an inch in stature (which, by the way, I've yet to find), my BMI has risen by an additional .8, now making it mandatory that I hang red caution flags from my jeans' hip pockets.

Still, I'm lighter than the average American adult female, who happens to be as tall as me but weighs in at 164 pounds. And that's *before* makeup.

Hence, I'm all for anything that will reduce my rump roast to a lean fillet, even if that means sleeping on the job and ... Zzz-zzz-zzz ... snort, snort ... Zzz-zzz-zzz ....

Oh, sorry about that. I hope you didn't mind that I took a little break. It was time for my booty rest.

Deedee's Supermarket Safety Guidelines

According to an insurance survey, 52 percent of all automobile accidents occur within five miles of home. No doubt, this is due to the close proximity of houses to supermarkets. I say this because shopping etiquette no longer exists among purveyors of produce. Today, it's every cart-pusher for herself, which has turned what used to be a leisurely experience into a hazardous mission. Those who aren't furious when they enter a supermarket often turn surly before they leave. And let's face it, there's nothing more dangerous than driving on streets occupied by disgruntled consumers armed with cantaloupes.

Right off, the situation could be improved if shoppers could be certain that their foods were free of harmful bacteria, poisons, and melamine. But beyond this we need a "Grocery Shoppers' Bill of Rights," so I've taken a stab at a first draft.

Grocery Shoppers' Bill of Rights

1. Every shopper shall have the right to push, pull, or otherwise maneuver his or her buggy through market

aisles at a self-determined pace. A safe stopping distance of at least three bread loaves should be maintained by cart drivers at all times.

2. Rolling baskets and any orbiting children shall travel in one direction, keeping the opposite side of the aisle free for passing. This does not include passing gas. Any person who "cuts the cheese" in a grocery aisle is obligated to prevent other shoppers from entering the odiferous zone by standing in place and fanning the air until any offensive smells have fully dissipated.

3. No grocery items shall be situated more than 5 feet above the floor. An empty bottom shelf providing a foothold does not constitute an acceptable substitution. Bare lower shelves are an attractive nuisance for "climb-and-getters." Parties with injuries sustained by reaching for items stored in violation of the 5-foot limit may be legally awarded treble damages and quadruple coupons.

4. Any grocery cart with a wobbly wheel shall be removed from service. Customers who encounter such defective buggies shall be authorized to immediately destroy said equipment.

5. Shoppers requiring more than one minute to deliberate over food purchases, e.g., to compare the sodium content of tomato soup to that of chicken and rice soup, shall be permitted to do so safely on Tuesdays between the hours of 9 and 11 a.m. At all other times, such customers are expected to circle and return to their product evaluation spot every 60 seconds until a final selection can be made.

6. To prevent customers from having to remove their wallets prior to making final payment, all grocery store scanners shall be capable of reading merchant-issued discount cards directly through handbags.

7. In accordance with the American Disabilities Act for Chronic Clippers, a special lane shall be made available for anyone who has five or more coupons.

8. All electronic data capture devices, including credit card swipe terminals, shall meet the Uniform Requirements for Left-handed Persons. Furthermore, such machines shall display data in a font size that can be easily read from a minimum of 2 feet away by persons who are both sober and capable of seeing well enough to legally drive.

9. Cashiers shall be required to dispense receipts, coupons, bills, and coins in separate exchanges, allowing customers sufficient time to place these items in their proper storage places. Cash register receipts, inclusive of any store or product advertisements and coupons, may not exceed a length equal to the number of items purchased multiplied by one-half inch nor the width of the register.

10. A minimum of 30 seconds shall be allowed between checkout transactions to permit buyers to put away their billfolds, assemble their children, and clear the checkout countertop before the next transaction begins. Violators of this rule shall be counseled after the first infraction and placed on probation after the second, and after any third breach, the offending cashier shall be swiftly disciplined by Taser gun.

God Save the Cantaloupe Queen

A cantaloupe was missing. I put away the groceries, grousing about those merry-go-round style bagging racks that spin my eggs, ice cream, and now, apparently, my produce off to the next patron. It must have been a fruit ball bonus day for someone—maybe someone who needed the beta-carotene worse than I did.

On a Friday afternoon, I had no intention of driving back to the supermarket for a $1.50 item. The matter would have been entirely different had this been something important like a chocolate bar. Since it was only a cantaloupe, and because my mind was preoccupied with a speech I had to soon deliver, I didn't give the MIA melon another thought.

My forthcoming presentation was about writing opinion columns, something I've done regularly, if not always accurately, for more than a decade. Nonetheless, I've always been a bit nervous about addressing business organizations. Anyone could be in the audience, possibly someone who's read something I've written.

Who was I to hold out myself as an expert? That is, on anything other than avoiding housework, taxes, and responsible journalism.

The title of my speech was "How to become an opinion page star." What the heck did that mean? How many guest columns would it take to make someone famous? Maybe just one, if the commentary focused on a hot issue such as smoking, dogs, or celebrity arrests.

On the day of my engagement, I chose to wear a peach-color pants suit. The ensemble looked professional enough, I reasoned. My hair, for once, was having a happy day. And not a single stress zit had decided to make an appearance along with me. I drew in a deep breath and considered what might be my worst-case scenario.

Relax. If I trip and fall or spill tea on my tablemate, no one will remember that a month from now.

That Tuesday morning I strolled to the garage carrying my briefcase of books. And that's when I noticed it, an odor I couldn't quite identify. Something out there reeked. Had my husband set a sack of trash in the garage and forgotten about it? Searching, I found nothing other than the usual strewn tools, paint cans, and prehistoric spiders. One of the arachnids waved and stepped aside for me.

Whatever the stench was, I didn't have time to ferret out its source. If I didn't leave right then, I'd risk being late for my appointment. I tugged open my vehicle door, and that's when it hit me: the methane from my missing melon. The cantaloupe had been in my car trunk all along—for four, sweltering days!

Now my auto smelled like it had suffered a collision with a sanitation truck. At the end of its route. On a 110-degree day. I tried lowering the windows, but I promptly aborted that action when it wrecked my hairdo.

My right eye twitched as I realized that my melon-colored apparel was absorbing the putrid, though strangely coordinating, fumes from my perished produce. By the time I made it to my meeting, I was sure to look like a fruit and smell like a farmer's market dumpster.

Upon arrival, I vigilantly scanned the audience. To my horror, among the attendees I noted a state senator, a county commissioner, and a newspaper publisher. Without question, though, I was the only star cantaloupe in the crowd.

If your grocery items should turn up missing, I'd advise an immediate search of your car trunk. And if you don't find what you're looking for, you might want to consider consuming more beta-carotene. I hear that cantaloupe is a good source when you can keep up with it.

The Truth About Barbecue and Burgers

It's no wonder there's so little agreement on the subject of barbecue. You can't even get everyone to similarly spell the word. I've seen signs that read "barbecue," "Bar-B-Q," and ones that simply used the acronym "BBQ," which I'm pretty sure stands for "burnt beyond question."

In Texas, where I'm from, we smoke and baste everything from pork to pizza. Our motto is, "If it can't be smothered in hickory sauce, then it ain't worth eating." We barbecue grill our beef and pork, potatoes and corn, and anything else that wanders too close to the outdoor cooker.

We like to think we're the ones who invented this process, though many claim otherwise. Seeing as how those folks aren't from Texas, we simply ignore them.

The origins of barbecue have long been disputed. Everyone from Native Americans to East Coast early colonists has received credit for developing this cooking method. Truth be told, the responsible party was probably a bored caveman who'd grown tired of eating the same old charbroiled mastodon every night.

To barbecue meats correctly, you must first sear the cuts at high temperatures—preferably somewhere near the flashpoint at which sand turns to glass. Then reduce the heat and slow-cook at about 250 degrees forever.

If you smoke or roast anything long enough, it will eventually become tender. Even armadillo. But who wants to eat a creature that can be hunted only in the dark, with an automobile? I don't recommend getting this creative.

The word "barbecue" can be either a noun or a verb. It is both the process and the end product of slow cooking and smoking meats. (Beware: The surgeon general has warned that puffing on too much pork may lead to a potbelly.)

I'm pretty sure the reason barbecuing caught on during the frontier days was because it met two beneficial needs. First, the men knew where their women were during hog-killing time (in the kitchen or smokehouse, barbecuing pork). And second, when the outdoor temperatures spiraled during the summer and threatened to turn the meat into buzzard bait, barbecue sauce covered up the taste. So when company said, "Mm-mm-mm. This barbecue sure is good. When did you slaughter this pig?" the cook could just smile and honestly reply, "Oh, the secret's in the sauce."

Today, nearly every southern family reunion includes barbecued meats of some kind. That's because barbecue has been scientifically found to reduce infighting. It's next to impossible to argue with a spare rib dangling from your lips. And there's no surer way to get kids to wash their hands than to make them lick their fingers.

The secret is in the sauce.

When it Comes to Grilling Burgers, Bubba Knows Best

In Texas, burgers are big business. We have burger wars during which restaurants compete for the championship title. Yet few commercial establishments can surpass the backyard summer staple better known as the Bubba Burger.

Bubbas consider charbroiling an act of manly competition. Do not challenge them in this matter or else you will find yourself on the wrong end of a set of barbeque tongs. Wise observers learn to quietly take note of these grilling masters' torching skills. Bubbas are experts when it comes to handling raw meat.

Having witnessed the creation of many a Bubba Burger, I'll share with you some chef secrets I've discovered. Here is a sure-fire method to produce the perfect patty:

Step 1: Start with the proper grade of beef. Use only ground round that is at least 36 percent fat. (It's no coincidence that "fat" and "flavor" both begin with the same letter.)

Add nothing but salt and pepper to your meat. Save the

A-1 and other sauces for beef purchased in identifiable shapes. Nobody likes a soupy, soggy set of buns.

Step 2: Between two sheets of wax paper, smash the patties into desired thicknesses (anywhere between a quarter-inch and the circumference of your mouth when fully open). Forgo the wax paper if you don't mind having your palms smeared with bacteria capable of producing fever, vomiting, and awareness for the Centers for Disease Control and Prevention.

Step 3: Heat your outdoor grill to the appropriate temperature. This should be somewhere between 500 degrees Fahrenheit and didn't-that-used-to-be-a-resin-patio-chair. This reminds me: Be sure to remove all lawn furniture from within a 50-foot radius of the grill.

Step 4: Place the patties on the cooking surface, close the grill cover, and do not open it again until you can no longer see the unit for the engulfing smoke and flames. At that time, throw back the lid and, using a spatula with a handle that is at least 5 feet long, flip the burgers. It's okay to use a shorter length implement as long as you're wearing a pair of asbestos mitts and a welder's mask.

Step 5: At the last minute, toss on a slice of cheese and hope that it melts before you've singed off all the hairs on your forearms. This should take about a .001 second if you've achieved the correct heating level. The cheese will form a protective shroud around the meat and prevent those succulent juices from escaping before they can be ingested, congealed, and transformed like magic into cardiologists' fees.

Step 6: Showcase the burgers on buns that are no more than 10 percent larger than the charcoaled meat. This requires buns that measure about half the size you think a real burger ought to be, which is where most end up after they've been sizzled to well dead, I mean done.

Now, sit back and enjoy that Bubba Burger. Try to ignore the dark plumes forming over your neighbor's back yard. Some folks will go to any length to win the burger war.

Wacky Water

Americans have insatiable appetites for silly products and services. We clamor for items that, short of savvy marketing, possess no natural demand. Consider, if you will, the true need for cashmere doggy sweaters, low-carb pastas, or special bra-fitting engagements.

The dog would probably rather receive $125 worth of rawhide treats. Real pasta lovers can tell the difference between spaghetti and freeze-dried glue. And our mothers and grandmothers somehow managed to support their breasts without ever once consulting a 19-year-old lingerie clerk.

Adding to the gusher of consumer products recently introduced, we now have enhanced bottled water. Along with fruity flavors and stomach-bloating fizz, drink makers have begun including vitamins and extra nutrients in their beverages. The marketing slogans for these thirst quenchers suggest bottled waters can not only hydrate and revitalize you, but they might also replace your spouse.

Here are a few of the ad headlines that caught my attention: "Water that never fakes it," "Water that works every time," and (drum roll) "Water with an IQ." Wow! Talk about selling the sizzle and not the beefcake!

I love the advertisements that hawk beverages for "active people." Who, exactly, are these energetic individuals? Other than sports jocks and UPS drivers, how many folks are so hyper that they can't stand still long enough to pour a drink from the tap?

And what's all this noise about replacing electrolytes? How can you even tell when you've lost them? I've never seen one.

If you want to earn my attention, then give me something to replenish collagen. At least I know when that's been depleted because I can see my chin double.

One Web site I visited boasted the names of baseball stars who endorse the company's vitamin enhanced sports drink. I don't get it. Why should I care what a baseball player guzzles? I mean, my son's dog can fetch a baseball. And he drinks from the toilet (the dog, that is, not my son).

Maybe I'm just more focused on inner wellbeing than external vitality. Still, that doesn't make me copy every guru's habit either. You know, some yogis seek the fountain of youth by swallowing their own urine.

It's possible that I'm too inert to understand the thirst for "fitness water." My idea of putting a body in motion is skipping my nap to get in some extra reading. So when I learned about this new water craze, I started thinking (one of my more strenuous activities) about how far this trend might go. What other kinds of enhancements might these beverage manufacturers offer? And shouldn't somebody address the needs of those who exhibit a more sedentary lifestyle?

After careful consideration, I came up with the following list of products and promotional brand names that hold potential:

Product	**Brand Name**
Water enhanced with Valium	Clearly Calm
Water combined with a laxative	H2Go
Water plus anti-diarrhea medication	Block-aid
Water and a sedative	Sparkless
Water containing muscle relaxers	Liqui-Limp
Water enhanced with Viagra	AquaRise
Water combined with antihistamines	NoNase
Water plus a daily birth control pill	Ocean Spay
Water and omega 3 oils	UpStream
Water with an aphrodisiac	Minute-Laid

When you think about it, the possibilities are frightening.

Making Vino

"Wouldn't it be fun to make our own wine," my husband, Jim, said, as if we were budding vintners instead of late-blooming fun seekers. "Here's a place where we can do it," he added, pointing to his computer screen.

"You can do it online?" I asked.

"No, you have to go downtown," he clarified.

I didn't want to drive into downtown Dallas because ... well, because it's in Dallas. But it was either do this or face eight loads of laundry. And I didn't want to discourage my normally preoccupied mate from suggesting new ideas for joint activities, so I agreed to become a vintner for the day.

Inside the winery a young man greeted us and offered to let us taste several wines. "The tastings are three for $5," he explained. "But you're not limited to three," he quickly assured.

We sat at a small bar and pored over a printed wine list, each of us placing a check mark next to the ones we thought sounded interesting. I assumed we'd compare notes and settle in on the similar varieties we'd both chosen. But when we cross-referenced our sheets, we'd picked different wines. So we agreed on a compromise: sample six wines instead of three.

By my fourth serving, I was ready to do a backstroke in one of the vats.

"Would you like to try to make one of these wines?" our server asked.

I draped my head on Jim's shoulder and slurred, "Whadda ya th-i-i-n-k, hon?"

He stared at me goo-goo-eyed and said, "Su-u-u-re. Why not?"

We giggled as we donned burgundy-colored aprons. Meanwhile, our host poured us another drink "on the house."

Standing over white plastic five-gallon buckets, we awaited further instructions.

First, we added several gallons of purified water to our containers. As I stared into the liquid, I noticed a hair had fallen from my head into the can. "Hey, look," I said. "I'm making Cabernet Savign-blond."

I fished out the strand and continued on.

The next purposeful ingredient we added was bentonite, a clay-like substance that is in no way related to Superman. Bentonite serves as a platform for the yeast to glob onto during the clarifying process. Right then, I took another swig of my drink and thought how I, too, could have used something to steady myself. I churned a paddle, turning my mixture into what looked like a muddy solution.

Next, it was time to add the grape juices, which our instructor offered to do for me, presumably because I was in no shape to shoot a stream of stain-producing liquids into anything smaller than, oh, say, a swimming pool.

Finally, we checked the sugar content with a hydrometer, a gadget that measures something or other I didn't quite understand. Our guide said the reading reflected a gravity of 1.1. "That's about twenty-five percent sugar," said the knowledgeable young man, "or about 14½ percent alcohol." His voice faded in and out of my awareness. "You'd be surprised how much difference you can tell between 14½ percent and 15 percent alcohol," he enthused.

"Oh, yeah," I agreed, thinking I'd surely been served the 15 percent version.

By the time I'd set some yeast sprinkles floating on the concoction's surface, I no longer cared about the color of the contents. This was way more fun than doing laundry!

"Now we'll add the woody flavor," said our guide. He handed me an envelope of what looked like fine potting soil but was, in fact, ground oak chips. I mixed the powder with water to form a paste and dumped it into the fun juice. Then we capped off the bucket of brew and sent it away to ferment for six to eight weeks.

Our new friend poured us another round to celebrate our successful completion. While I'd love to tell you what happened next, I honestly don't remember.

Cooking with Deedee

Deedee Divine's Best Pumpkin Pie

It's possible to make a pumpkin pie from a real pumpkin (as opposed to a canned one). But like natural childbirth, why would anyone want to do that?

Perhaps a pie baked from the wholesome natural gourd tastes immensely better than one scooped from a container. Certainly, the original cooking process is more time-consuming and messy. However, it could offer a culinary connection to our nation's foremothers. And since I still had a fully intact pumpkin left over from Halloween, I decided to find out.

Through research I discovered that the first Thanksgiving feast hadn't included anything sweet, unless you count dried fruits and lucrative food swaps. In exchange for the five deer (or about 200 pounds of venison) the American Indians brought to the table, the pilgrims shared with them some roasted fowl. This worked out so well that later the settlers tricked their friends into trading them land for a bunch of casinos.

Armed with only the vaguest instructions, I ventured into

the kitchen to re-enact an early American custom.

My daughter Laura agreed to be my accomplice. "Let me see what the recipe says," I said to her. "I've no clue what I'm doing."

The guidelines suggested only that I should start with a two- to four-pounder. Lifting the jack-o-lantern size melon in front of me, I speculated it weighed slightly more.

"Put it on the bathroom scale," Laura advised.

According to that gauge, the pumpkin weighed 13 pounds. But I dismissed the apparent conflict.

Stabbing at the leathery rind with a butcher knife, I narrowly missed puncturing my spleen. "Maybe you should get out your electric knife," my helper cautioned.

"Either that or your dad's chainsaw," I replied.

By the time I finished sawing the gourd, I'd coated the countertops, electrical outlets, and both our shirts in yellow-orange pulp.

A cloud of odors emanated from the freshly cut fruit, creating a stench that smelled like mildewed towels and Roquefort cheese. Between gags, Laura scraped at the stringy orange mess laced with seeds. We both wanted to puke.

"Just think," she said. "Once upon a time, somebody smelled this and actually thought it might make a good pie."

After an hour of baking, the meat of our work had roasted tender. It was time to remove the skin and puree the soggy yellow chunks. But the pumpkin's texture demanded prolonged mashing, which naturally required me to use an ancient cooking tool known as a food processor.

My pie recipe called for 12 ounces of cooked pumpkin, so I stopped blending at 10 cups. (Note to cooks: A 13-pound pumpkin yields enough goop to fill a gasoline tanker truck.)

"You have to make the crust from scratch," Laura

enthused. "Using a store-bought one just wouldn't do. Not after all this."

She was right, though I hated to admit it.

Six hours after our official start time, I removed from the oven a perfectly ordinary, questionably prepared, and thoroughly unattractive desert. My feet throbbed, my kitchen reeked, and my sink overflowed. I'd burned up an electric knife, a food processor, half my day, and the last of my patience.

Now I know why the pilgrims' feast didn't include this traditional desert. If they'd served pumpkin pie, Thanksgiving would've lasted at least two days longer. And the meat might have rotted before the pies were done.

Take it from me; the best way to make a pumpkin pie is to let your grocer bake it.

Giblet Gravy and Grandma

Thanksgiving is about more than just food and sharing. It's a time of personal reflection, a day to show gratitude to God and a chance to ponder important questions—like, "What would happen if nobody made a green bean casserole this year?" and, "Who's responsible for the woefully inadequate 'low-flow' toilet?"

Officially though, Thanksgiving is a holiday that's somewhat of a misnomer. There's no shortage of labor around here. It takes all week for me to clean the cat hair out of my kitchen, not to mention the effort that's required to baste and roast a bird whose breast eclipses mine.

First, I have to find all the parts—which are never hidden in logical places. Oh, sure, there's an obvious hole on each end of the carcass. But the heart, liver, and other innards have been stuffed inside the neck opening. And the neck has been relocated to the rear cavity. This causes me to wonder what that turkey might have been doing right there at the last. Was he thinking, "Hey, something doesn't seem right. I better take a look up my ...."

Another problem is that stubby, fleshy appendage jutting out the bottom of the fowl. Does anyone really eat this? I can't imagine a guest saying, "Whoa, man, save me the turkey tail. That's my favorite piece!" Poultry producers ought to remove that nasty reminder of what we're really stuffing.

Speaking of gross encounters, as far as I'm concerned giblet gravy ranks right up there with pork brains (which, by the way, I've never tried). If a food can't be named to correspond with some part of the standard anatomy, then I don't want to serve it. Show me a bird's giblet. You can't because there's no such thing. "Giblet" is simply another word for "guts."

My husband enjoys "gut gravy." So I stifle my objections and do my duty. Yep, I let him make it.

Families often disagree over how best to cook their Toms. The mass marketing of turkey fryers has further added to today's choices. We can roast, smoke, deep-fry, honey glaze, beer can skewer, or prepare our birds the rural Texas way, which is to say, barbecued straight over the burn barrel.

At my house, the main course more closely resembles road kill by the time anyone thinks to document Thanksgiving. There's nothing left but skeletal remains when Grandma typically commands, "Y'all line up over here for a five-generation photo." This causes us all to scramble into a haphazard jumble of bloated bellies. Those who are still capable of sprinting will then run to flank the most rotund person in the family. By posing sideways, they further make themselves appear thinner. These rituals seldom change.

This year, we'll roast our bird, like always. The turkey platter will be late arriving on the table owing to my chronic failure to calculate sufficient thawing time. Children will race behind my back as I hoist heaping pans of dressing from the oven, and I'll suffer burns that no one notices. Later, the sink disposal might erupt or the toilets could clog.

Nobody, however, will snap that five-generation photo.

Grandma passed away in 2006. I will miss her holiday contributions and her shutterbug tendencies. Whenever she took a family picture, I was always the most popular person in the room. Relatives practically raced to stand next to me.

You Are What I Eat

A slew of medical research confirms that my lifestyle, despite my mental state, is perfectly healthy. However, according to the latest studies, your behaviors should be my concern.

Yes. That's right. Findings from a study published in *The New England Journal of Medicine* suggest that you're not only what you eat, but also what your friends eat, too. In other words, when you get fat, so do I.

Researchers determined that when people put on weight, that increase in heft affects their buddies as well as their bodies. By analyzing records from the Framington Heart Study, scientists found that, on average, a 17-pound weight gain in one individual will cause a close friend to put on 5 pounds. Given that ratio, someone I know must have packed on 150 pounds!

But here's the most mind-boggling part of this obesity study: It took researchers 32 years to figure out what most of us can determine from one good party. Overweight people often have chubby chums.

This brings me to a simple question: Would you please go on a diet?

I don't mean to be insulting. It's just that, assuming this

process works in reverse, if you reduce your caloric intake then I won't have to. And if for the greater good of humanity someone has to be on food restrictions, I'd prefer that this person be you.

In other medical news, chocolate has been found to reduce blood pressure and caffeine has been discovered to decrease sun-damaged skin cells.

In a study that examined the effects of exercise combined with caffeine intake in rodents (which do not closely resemble man, but chimps would have been smart enough to demand Starbucks), mice that were both active and stimulated by caffeine gained protection from sun exposure. When both voluntary exercise and caffeine consumption were present, hairless mice suffered fewer damaged skin cells than vermin that were more sluggish (or otherwise preoccupied with reproduction) and drank decaf.

I find it suspicious anytime the words "voluntary" and "exercise" appear in the same sentence. Without caffeine, I suspect the thumb-size subjects would have been much less inclined toward impromptu wheel spinning.

So the question remains: Is caffeine really good for you? To confirm this, more funding will surely be necessary. In the meantime, I can happily defend my two-dark-chocolate-squares-and-four-sodas-per-day habit. And since I have no compulsion to exercise, there's little reason to add workouts to my regimen.

Don't you just love it when science hands you everything you need to continue living exactly the way you have been?

Along these same lines, not long ago, I learned that limited consumption of red wine can be good for cardiovascular health. Experts advise women to restrict their wine intake to one drink and men to two per day. Oddly, there's no mention of the permissible number of drinks per night.

Additionally, a Harvard study of 81,000 women drawn from the Nurses' Health Study concluded that, of 17 liquids tested, wine most effectively reduced the risk of kidney stones (by 59 percent). This research further supports the benefits of moderate drinking, as well as offers a possible explanation for nurse staffing shortages.

So why doesn't someone conduct a study of the effects of wine and chocolate on journalists? Why not pick a profession from which the research participants won't be missed?

I'd include more medical findings here, but right now it's time for my Dr Pepper and candy bar break. You, on the other hand, might want to consider fasting—which would be the noble thing to do. The sacrifices you make may very well prevent the suffering of others.

THE CUSTOMER IS ALWAYS RILED

Letter House of Horrors

On the list of places I'd rather avoid than visit, right after federal prison I'd add the U.S. Post Office. Occasionally, though, I have to ship packages from what I call The Letter House of Horrors.

During a recent visit—actually, during every visit I've ever made to this torture tunnel—only three postal windows were open for operation. And the wait line couldn't have been any worse if the joint had been serving free margaritas. Sadly, though, they weren't.

In a far greater case of government waste, I've learned that most post office stations are equipped with at least six teller windows. The possibility of these areas ever being fully staffed, however, is about as likely as the chance of Oprah Winfrey going bankrupt.

An employee emerged from a concealed area and sauntered out into the main lobby. She shuffled past me and drawled, "Does anyone here have a package or certified letter to pick up?"

No one budged.

Witnessing the long line of broiling patrons, the carrier shrugged and then ambled out of sight.

At an open window, a lady stood discussing all the possible permutations and combinations for shipping a camera—which, by the way, she hadn't bothered to confine to a box. A few feet from her, two women, one behind and the other in front of the counter, looked as though they might be joyfully sharing family news. And at the third station, a lengthy discussion had ensued over more serious matters—possibly, commemorative stamps.

In front of me, a man collapsed into a heap on the narrow bar installed to keep the rest of us at a safe distance from postal counter loiterers. I heard him mumbling what sounded like a prayer for deliverance.

Why were all these people hogging the postal windows? Couldn't they see the trail of exasperated cell phone users waiting behind them?

The single-file line of patrons crept forward as I stared at my sandals to keep from thinking homicidal thoughts. Parched with thirst and suppressing the urge to shout, "For the love of GOD!" I observed my toenails grow a full inch.

The guy directly in front of me looked like he might be about to weep. "Can I just get stamps from that machine out there?" he whined to the worker who'd earlier disappeared. She'd returned to again incite the crowd.

"Sure," she said. "But it will only take a credit card."

A credit card? Half the folks in line with me were mailing money orders! If they had a credit card, they wouldn't be here!

When I finally made my way to the next available window, the man who waited on me glanced at my parcel and inquired, "Are you mailing anything perishable, hazardous or restricted?"

Through dry lips I croaked, "It's a book." I wanted to yell,

"Can't you see that I'm suffering from dehydration?" But instead, I said, "That's why I stamped it Media Mail."

Good grief. If my package had contained anything perishable, then it would have already rotted. And if there'd been anything hazardous in that manila envelope, I probably would have used it on myself.

Dining Advice from Deedee

I used to enjoy dining out, but not anymore. These days, it seems my restaurant choices have fallen into two categories best summarized as "Bring-Your-Platinum-Card" or "Bring-Your-Ear-Plugs." And since triple-digit dining doesn't fit my budget, I'm relegated to eating unremarkable meals inside I-Couldn't-Care-Less Steakhouse and the Bite Me Café. Okay, I'll admit I made up those names. But you probably know the places I mean.

Most businesses will do whatever they can to attract and keep their patrons. Like me, you've probably wondered why many restaurants seem indifferent to their guests. Surely there's some bizarre marketing gimmick behind their cavalier attitudes toward customers. Maybe crowded seating, mediocre foods, and overpriced beverages have proven successful somewhere else—like Mars or Manhattan—and these eateries are only following a trend. All I know is that during a recent restaurant visit I decided the following:

- Hostesses will not offer you booth seating unless you demand it. Waiters don't like to be limited in directional approaches they can use to interrupt intimate conversations.

- If you are seated in a private nook, it will be located directly across from a vocal toddler who's using his tray table as a chicken nugget launch pad.

- Restaurants are poorly lit so they can shunt more power to their air conditioning systems. Thus, all standard light bulbs have been replaced with the energy efficient kind typically found in clothes dryers. If you plan to order from the menu, remember to bring your night-vision goggles.

- The house wine will taste like swill and average $8 a glass. Important advisory: When ordering wine, do not expect to receive a full goblet. Fearing overflow, your sight-challenged server will pour only half the drink you've purchased.

- Menu listings won't always identify seafood entrées by type of fish. Generic names like "Catch of the Day" and "Bay Stew" better distract diners from environmental issues. Who really know what a scallop is, anyway?

- Salad dressing rations are now in effect due to the high cost of transportation. I'm not sure how gasoline and ranch dressing are related, but there must be some connection. Anyhow, expect no discernable evidence of moisture on your salad.

- All dishes must be returned to the kitchen within 15 minutes or the diner will start serving meals on cardboard coasters. Those who fail to comply will suffer the shame of having to confess their plans to polish off everything on their own as well as their spouse's plate.

- If you're fortunate enough to consume your full meal within the allotted timeframe, your waiter will exclaim, "My, we were hungry tonight, weren't we?" The only suitable response to this is, "I don't know. I didn't get to see what you ate."

How Well Do I Need to Know My Food Server?

In search of a good meal, I found a new friend. I could tell he earnestly sought to make a good first impression and an intimate connection, though initially the only thing I'd planned to give him was my appetite.

It was a Monday, on one of those holidays that only retailers in need of excuses for sales events tend to acknowledge. Six hours past our breakfasts, my mate and I were famished, so we stopped in a chain restaurant known for its exhaustive menu of casual food and expensive beverages. We were seeking purely physical rather than emotional sustenance—because that's just the kind of shallow people we are.

When our waiter arrived, he crouched low next to our table, his eyes at breast level, and greeted us with an enthusiastic, "Hi, guys."

What a relief. Most assuredly he had not been staring down my neckline. Otherwise my gender would have been obvious. It's refreshing to find a young man who'll simply look you straight in the sternum.

Just as I readied myself to blurt out my order, our host asked, "So-o-o, how's your weekend been, so far?"

I considered sharing that I'd been incapacitated for the past two days with allergies and had ingested enough meds to supply an entire Olympic team. In fact, I was fairly certain my pharmaceutical purchases had prompted a nationwide shortage of antihistamines. Before I could muster the words to convey this, my spouse offered his idea of an informative response.

"Fine," he replied.

I shot my tablemate a look. Surely he realized this waiter's attempt at small talk stemmed from the polite man's longing to know us better.

"Can I start y'all off with some artichoke dip and chips or maybe fried onion rings today?" asked the attendant.

"No," said my husband. "I believe we'd just like to order our meal. I'm trying to diet."

"Diet?" Our server exhibited a shocked expression. "Neither of you looks like you need to diet."

It was a shame this guy was too old to adopt. But maybe I could invite him to our next family get-together. Surely our girls would like him. They'd probably think he was "buff" and that his choppy haircut was "hot." Possibly one of them would even date and eventually marry him.

"Well," I interjected, "at your age, you don't have to worry about such things. But when you pass a certain point, you have to be more careful about calories."

"Oh, come on," said the fellow in charge of our food order. "You guys aren't *that* old."

When our broiled chicken and salmon dinners arrived, our soon-to-be-son-in-law remarked, "Boy, I sure hope you're both hungry."

Not wanting to embarrass him, I refrained from pointing out that most restaurant patrons are hankering for a meal.

After all, he was only trying to maintain the rapport he'd already built with us. Studying his bone structure, I wondered how he might feel about children.

When our check arrived, I was sitting there hoping this guy might be moonlighting as a waiter while he was finishing medical school. Setting down the black tray that contained our bill, the future father of our grandchildren jutted one hand toward my spouse and said, "It's been my pleasure to serve you today." And in a male bonding sort of way, the two exchanged a hearty handshake.

Then our newfound family addition extended the same gesture to me. However, I couldn't bring myself to accept it. Goodbyes just shouldn't have to be this hard.

7 Habits of Highly Self-Absorbed People

At the beginning of a new year, it's normal for individuals—people who are more focused than I—to search for meaning, reflect on the past, and plan for the future. But the truth is, the future never really arrives. It just keeps moving further away.

Thousands who wish to take charge of tomorrow, however, flock to sellers of self-improvement books, tapes, DVDs, teleconferences, and cyber seminars. These hopefuls attend fire-walking, board-busting, rope-swinging, and pretzel-twisting performances that demonstrate the power of mind over body—the power of the performers' ideas to send audience members' hands reaching for their wallets.

Yes, I'll admit that I've attended a few of these self-improvement seminars and teleconferences (and you can see how well they've worked for me). If you're thinking of doing the same, this tidbit could save you tens or even thousands of dollars. Most self-help speakers' messages can be summed up in one sentence: The keys to success can be yours if you buy my book, CD, or DVD.

If you purchase one of these products, in all probability,

you will then be instructed to attend a teleconference or contract for a coaching session in which you will be 100 percent guaranteed to improve your mentor's life.

To save you time and expense, I'd like to offer you, for free (Well, okay, maybe not exactly free, but included with the price of this book.), the "7 Habits of Highly Self-Absorbed People."

You might ask what qualifies me to provide this kind of advice. Well, I'm as much an authority on personal growth as anyone. Within the past 30 days I've grown at least five pounds!

7 Habits of Highly Self-Absorbed People

1. **Set goals.** Establish goals and write them down. Set them anywhere you please, as long as you can find them again without calling Admin 9-1-1.

2. **Spout positive statements.** Tell yourself and the world how wonderful you are. Distort the truth if you have to. Affirm (which is a fancy way of saying "pretend") that your desires have already been realized. Be specific, though. If you simply announce, "Abundance is mine, now," you could gain as much as an inch in girth overnight.

3. **Network.** Attend every social, business, and civic function you can. And never, ever, give anyone your full attention. Be on constant lookout for the next potential client or purveyor of your services. If you spot a camera, position yourself as close as possible to the photographer.

4. **Spin your personal accomplishments.** Inflate your

achievements when discussing them with others. Did you buy your child a cell phone for Christmas? If so, you just "signed a deal with a major telecommunications firm." Got the idea? Here's another example: I attended an Oprah seminar, so, technically, I "appeared with Oprah." Hey, we were both inside the same convention center.

5. **Go the extra mile.** Always give more than is expected. This is best done by surrounding yourself with those who expect very little—preferably other successful, self-absorbed people. They understand the game you're playing.

6. **Demonstrate gratitude.** Acknowledge those who've helped you attain your goals (especially the Creator). Don't forget the people who worship your friendship as if it might actually one day prove beneficial.

7. **Be generous.** Generously give of your time, talents, and resources, and whenever possible, turn your good deeds and actions into photo opportunities. Share what you've learned with others, which leads me to this final thought: Buy my books.

Stay tuned for important information about upcoming seminars.

ROMANCE &
OTHER MYTHS

There's Nothing Romantic About February

Let's talk about love, shall we? I consider myself an expert on this topic because I can correctly pronounce *agape* (both the version that designates affection and the one that describes how my kids leave our doors). I try not to brag about this too much, though, so I won't get stuck writing an advice column where women ask why their dogs never seem to want to cuddle. Or maybe that was their husbands who didn't want to snuggle. No, wait. I think it was their husbands who wouldn't stop hugging their dogs.

It's high time someone started a campaign to reschedule Valentine's Day. This holiday needs to be moved to a warmer, or at least a more arousing, month. I mean, there's nothing enchanting about flaking skin, flannel sheets, and flu season—unless you have some really weird fetishes.

According to the few Valentine's Day authorities I consulted (Howstuffworks.com, my *Chase's Calendar of Events* book, and Mom), there is little consensus on what we're even celebrating—besides a couple saints who were beheaded on this day in history.

Some suggest this unofficial holiday originated with a

pagan fertility celebration, Lupercalia. That certainly makes sense, though, for me, the word "fertility" has a way of putting an immediate damper on any desires to party. During the Roman feast of Lupercalia, women wrote love letters, like they do now to Dr. Phil, and cast them into a large urn. Hopeful men withdrew one note apiece from the "love lottery pottery," and then each participant affectionately pursued his letter's author for the remainder of the year. (Important note: Because of the expected brevity of these couplings, there was no such thing as divorce in this society, and no one's chariot was ever once vandalized.)

Eventually, in an act of rebellion, ladies decided they'd rather select their suitors than take their chances on being paired with a guy named Gladius Permanus, who was rumored to be perpetually in an amorous mood.

But as I previously mentioned, there are few historical facts upon which to base the origins of Valentine's Day. So I started wondering what other, perhaps less obvious, reasons there might be for why we celebrate this holiday in the dead of winter. Here are 10 possibilities that I came up with:

1. To attract male participation, Valentine's Day had to be scheduled after football season ended.

2. Candy salesmen needed something to offset all the dieting during the beginning of the year.

3. Fewer shopping days in February caused retailers to favor this month.

4. Religious leaders demanded the holiday occur before Lent so they wouldn't have to give up you-know-what.

5. The Irish had dibs on their own saint's day in March.

6. The IRS caused too many "performance issues" in April.

7. Weddings overcrowded June—when everyone was already paired off.

8. Greeting card companies didn't want to cannibalize their Easter, Mother's Day, and Father's Day card sales.

9. July was already "hot" enough.

10. Men complained that ladies required SOME incentive to shave their legs before spring!

Despite the compelling reasons I've cited for honoring Valentine's Day in February, I still think we should change this holiday to a more suitable time like, say, maybe May 1. Spring is the season for lovers. February is the month to acknowledge dead presidents and department store white sales.

Besides, during wintertime, it's going to require substantially more than a card and a box of candy to get me to shave my legs.

DEEDEE'S TIPS ON CHOOSING CHOCOLATES

Valentine's Day, though joyful for romantics, can prove hopelessly confusing for some. Not everyone is fortunate enough to be in a positive relationship on February 14. And for those who aren't, these can be troubling times. Even people who are casually dating struggle to get through the day without sending the wrong message.

Not yet sure if he or she is "the one"? Then I recommend a quick jaunt out of town. Nothing else can ensure this occasion won't wreck your future. One false move, one misconstrued card inscription, one wrong-colored flower, and you could find yourself committing to the kind of relationship you never intended.

If you think I'm kidding, just ask my husband. He gave me a necklace on our first Valentine's Day together. Two months later we were engaged.

Guys struggling to choose appropriate gifts for their sweethearts should simply buy chocolates. But pay attention to the details. White chocolate won't take you very far. Milk chocolate is better.

And if you want to win a gal's goodness, opt for imported, dark cocoa truffles. An Italian study revealed that women who eat chocolate are more sexually active than those who don't similarly indulge. This definitively explains why women on diets don't smile.

Females love chocolate because it contains caffeine and other ingredients known to stimulate arousal and trigger pleasure centers in the brain, and possibly elsewhere. However, you must be careful when selecting a container. It's critical that you pick the right size. The shape, color, and morsel quantity often affect the recipient's desires. Chocolates come in red, pink, and yellow heart-shaped boxes. Yet beware: Assortments run the full spectrum, from the smallest six-ounce sampler to the five-pound who-needs-a-man bulk carton.

Personally, I think it's best to appeal to all the senses, so I'd recommend the chocolates to perk up her taste buds and lilac scented soaps and candles to enchant her olfactory receptors. Buy your lady a silk robe so she'll feel luxurious.

For visual intrigue, give her a photo of you doing something sexy, like helping with the laundry or taking out the trash. And finally, sidle up close and whisper in her ear, "I paid off the MasterCard."

If that doesn't work, hold a mirror underneath her nose—to see if she's breathing.

Vanishing Valentine

One of the first rules of romance is that you must never leave your date alone on Valentine's night. Yet last year, that's exactly what happened to me. I was abandoned. Jim left me to eat dinner all by myself, at home, in front of the television, while he was out of town on business. And you know what else that meant? Yep. I had to clean the cat litter box.

Okay, before you start thinking that I'm married to a philanderer, I should tell you that's not the case. I'm hitched to a man whose employer couldn't care less about love. The company recruits from a university that exhibits similar disregard. This institution of higher learning conducts its annual recruiting event on Valentine's Day, and my guy had drawn the short straw to be an interviewer.

I tried not to think too long about how I was home with the cat while Jim sat a state away, staring into the baby blues of some campus babe and asking her how she might improve corporate internal controls.

One week earlier we'd traveled to Los Cabos, Mexico. Knowing we'd be separated for several days around Valentine's Day, we'd decided to spend some time together beforehand.

Excitedly, we anticipated observing the annual migration of whales. However, at the last minute, we'd both come down with a horrid case of the flu. Sick and feverish, we managed to make our flight. But in Los Cabos ... well, let's just say whenever Jim yelled, "There she blows," he wasn't referring to whales.

I've been thinking about how my hubby might compensate this year for last year's solo Valentine's Day. "Fly me to Paris for a candlelight dinner," I suggested.

"Why can't we just drive?" he asked. "It's only about two hours from here."

"Paris, France," I corrected. I thought for a moment and then made another stab. "Or maybe we could go to our favorite cabin in the Hill Country."

"Actually, I've got something I need to tell you," he confessed. "LSU is holding its recruiting event over Valentine's Day again this year."

"You had to do it last year!" I whined. "Don't even tell me they're suggesting you go again this year. Uh-uh. Nope. Not fair. It's somebody else's wife's turn to dine alone."

"My boss says he doesn't want to do it," my vanishing valentine insisted. "What am I supposed to say?"

"Just say NO."

"I can't do *that*!"

"Why not? Everybody else seems to get away with it."

I searched for a Valentine's present to soothe my slights. So, just for grins, I did some online research to see what male-oriented Web sites recommended giving a woman on this special day. Here's what I found:

Type of Relationship	**Suitable Gift**
Low-level commitment	Cards and flowers
High future expectations	Sexy blouse or eveningwear
Friends who "know" each other	Sexy lingerie or "toys"
Committed marriage	Silk sheets

The first thing I noticed about this list is that it doesn't recommend the man actually stick around once he's bestowed these gifts. Under the heading "committed marriage," I'd think being home overnight might be the first item of importance. Silk sheets can be awfully cold when you sleep on them all by yourself, or so I've heard.

What I'd like for Valentine's Day is simply to have my spouse remain home with me. And if that's asking too much, then he'd better hire some young hunky guy to come clean out the cat litter box.

A Time to Remember

"Do you mean to tell me that Valentine's Day is just a Hallmark holiday that somebody made up?" Jim cried. "There's not even a historical basis behind it?"

"Well, there sort of is," I replied. "It has something to do with a couple of saints who were beheaded on February 14."

"Whoa! That'll sure take the urge to merge right out of a fellow," he said, "but what's that got to do with sending cards to your lover?"

I knew what would happen if I elaborated on this subject. He was looking for any excuse he could find to relieve himself of Valentine's Day expectations.

"Valentine's is still a week away, and already roses have

doubled in price," declared my budget-minded hubby.

"And how would you know that?" I pressed, realizing that he followed the floral commodities markets about as closely as I monitored my auto maintenance schedule (which is to say, not at all).

He took his seat at the breakfast table and then admitted, "I stopped at the grocery store a few days ago, and I was going to get you some roses—until I saw the price. And then I decided, Valentine's Day being only a week away and all, to wait."

His first mistake was to have confessed that he'd thought about purchasing flowers and yet hadn't followed through. The second was to have revealed he didn't think I deserved a bouquet twice in the same month.

Perhaps he caught a glimpse of my expression, which fell somewhere between mild irritation and I-sure-hope-you-don't-expect-to-sleep-in-the-same-bed-with-me-tonight, because he quickly reached across the table and tenderly grasped my hands.

"Hon, you don't need cards and flowers to know that I love you," he cooed, "when I can just look in your eyes and hold your hands and say something meaningful from my heart."

I studied his face and spotted that dead giveaway twinkle he gets in his eyes every time he's conning me. "It's not gonna work," I said, shaking my head. "I'm still going to need a card, dinner, and flowers."

"Darn! I thought I had you that time!" he said, freeing me from his clutch. When he finally stopped hee-hawing like a mule, he pulled himself together and added, "Seriously, remember that time we sent the kids away for the evening, and I brought you that beautiful arrangement, the night we ate dinner by the fireplace and ...."

I nodded vigorously, indicating I recalled the evening

perfectly. It had been one of our best celebrations ever. I'd made a cheese fondue and some chocolate-covered strawberries. He'd brought home a stunning mixed bouquet in a cobalt blue, Italian glass vase, one he'd purchased from a real florist shop—the kind where they don't also sell beer and toilet bowl cleansers. If he was suggesting we plan another night like this one, I would willingly compromise on the dinner plans.

My Romeo shrugged and said, "Then why don't you just remember it AGAIN?" Now he was braying at full volume. "Why do we have to keep repeating these things?"

The next night, when he came home from work, I remained in my office for several minutes before greeting him. When I ventured out, I gave him a hug.

"What's for dinner?" he asked.

"Remember when I made you that homemade chicken lasagna that you just loved, and we had that great wine and ...?"

Excitedly he shook his head.

"Well, it looks like you're going to have to remember it *again*—because tonight I didn't cook!"

Wedding Sparkle

One of the many advantages of growing older is that I seldom get invited to weddings. Most of my friends, colleagues, and acquaintances have either already married or abolished the idea as being hopeless, hazardous, or potentially fatal—especially to prospective partners.

Though I'm happily espoused to my own Mr. Right, I shudder at the sight of a wedding invitation the way I would quake over a letter from the IRS. Before I've fully opened the embossed envelope, arrhythmia sets in. I can feel my throat constrict to fiber-optic proportions and shoulders rise to meet my earlobes. Within seconds, I'm compelled to prayer: "Dear Lord, I sure hope you've guided these two lovers to register at Target."

Weddings are expensive, not just for the bride's parents but also for the guests. Being color-coded gala affairs, these events dictate specific attire. This means that, in all likelihood, the attendees will need to spring for new duds and maybe some odd shade of shoes to match. And if participants aren't quick on the draw when choosing their gifts, they'd better be prepared to spend like their last name is Trump.

By the time I typically make my way to the department

stores to examine the wedding registry list, there's nothing left to buy but 12-piece settings of platinum flatware or Waterford Crystal table lamps. I wish all the presents would get opened at the reception so I could find out exactly who keeps beating me to the tea towels and Tupperware.

Frankly, most weddings are planned backwards, from the rehearsal dinner right down to the reception. Wouldn't it be nice if the committed couple hosted an appreciation dinner for the folks who raised them, for the people who provided the duo with their earliest examples of what to look for (or avoid) in a romantic union?

I can't believe more dads don't protest the idea of paying for their daughters' nuptials. Don't these men realize that they're sending the wrong message to their future sons-in-law? Starting the guy off with a $10,000+ subsidy is just flat encouraging the groom to expect more where that came from.

I have other complaints, too. If you think about it, most of those professional photos could be captured before, rather than after, the service. Forget all that hooey about hiding the bride before the ceremony. Such practices have never been about preventing bad luck. Somebody simply thought that by separating the wedding pair prior to their vows, there'd be greater opportunity for either one to make a last-minute escape.

After the band starts, the first dance is normally reserved for the wedding couple. However, that slow spin ought to be followed by a second one for those who previously clothed, fed, and successfully shuffled the bride and groom from their dole. These folks should proudly occupy the dance floor, salute each other with a collective "high-five," and then perform a shimmy-shake to James Brown's "I Feel Good."

During the betrotheds' departure well-wishers should skip all that rice-throwing and bubble-blowing. Newlyweds need to be showered with glitter to prolong the sparkle. Soon enough the clock will strike midnight, when fancy gowns and expensive suits turn into ordinary jeans and sweats, party music fades to the cries of needy children, and husbands and wives who once briefly resembled royalty better favor pumpkins.

Deedee's Rules for Marital Bliss

Getting hitched is actually pretty darn easy. It's the living together and having to like each other for so long that presents problems. Nevertheless, if you follow these simple rules, you'll find that keeping the knot tied will be less of a challenge:

Deedee's Rules for a Successful Marriage

- If you and your other half must ride in the same vehicle, consider blindfolding the non-driving partner to reduce conflict. Spouses who bark orders at their motoring mates cause hypertension, accidents, and sudden disappearances.

- Agree in advance on important matters such as the division of chores, any financial investment decisions, and time dedicated to televised sports.

- Don't share a joint bank account if you have separate ideas about recordkeeping. For example: Your mate believes every check should be immediately recorded when written, but you think the best way to determine your bank balance is to ask a teller.

- Recognize that it is less important who pays the bills than whose salary will be used to make the payments.

- Never go to sleep mad; you could wake up homicidal.

- Men, please understand that intimacy involves more than asking your partner to scratch your back.

- Ladies, realize that guys are not clairvoyant. If you want more touch, you'll have to explain that you'd like your hubby to provide this *after* he's put down the remote.

- Give each other at least one compliment each day. My husband likes to tell me, "You spend more money than anyone I know," and I enjoy pointing out, "You're the most unobservant man I've ever met."

- Accept flatulence as a sign of relationship comfort. No longer concerned with putting on airs, contented spouses are prone to expel some now and again.

- Spend equal time visiting with each partner's family—unless one set of parents is particularly rich and generous, in which case you will want to invite them to accompany you on all your vacations.

- Invest in a set of cordless, wireless TV headphones. Love means never having to say, "Will you turn that thing down!" which, by the way, is not a question.

- Resist the urge to criticize each others' habits unless these annoyances are, a.) harmful, b.) illegal, or c.) insane.

For instance, if your mate squeezes the last dollop of toothpaste from the tube, it's no big deal. But if he or she licks the final drop of goo from the cap and then swallows it—the toothpaste, but especially if the cap goes too—it's time to speak out.

- Refrain from using certain phrases that can trigger arguments. To be safe, consider eliminating from your vocabulary the word "savings."

- Respect each others' privacy in the privy. In other words, don't solicit a morning "poo" report like you're checking the day's weather forecast. And never, ever yell from the bathroom, "Hon, you gotta come see this!"

The mystery of what keeps two people together is sometimes hard to crack. A great deal of trial and error went in to devising these rules, so I figured I needed to pass them along. It's the least I could do to promote nuptial bliss.

September Mourn

Labor Day is a time when many people think of vacations, picnics, parties, and family cookouts. But for me, the holiday evokes visions of matrimony.

My husband and I decided to marry on a significant date, one that might remind us of the type commitment we were making. Having both been previously divorced, we understood that marriage is more than just sharing the same bed, meals, and expenses. It means also divvying up closet space and learning how to considerately use the same toilet. That's why we got hitched on Labor Day.

In hindsight, this holiday might not have been the best choice for our ceremony.

Metaphorically speaking, it doesn't bode well that this date falls smack dab in the middle of hurricane season. And there's something disconcerting about being wed when our state's game department has just declared open season on the symbol of peace.

However, if we should ever forget our anniversary, it's reassuring to know we'll be reminded by the gunfire.

Perhaps a better time for a wedding would have been Halloween. After all, weren't we both wearing disguises?

I thought he was a guy with superb manners and active listening skills. He'd been fooled into thinking I was a gal who'd always remain thin and employed. Talk about being tricked!

But we'll always have the illusions.

My partner, Jim, and I married inside a home that we'd spent the past 30 days remodeling. I kind of figured it like this. If two people can survive living with Cheech and Chong for contractors, being lost for entire days inside a home improvement store, and groping their way through clouds of Sheetrock dust, then they can likely weather in-laws, parenting, and shared closets.

I hadn't counted on how important it was that one of us be proficient at mundane chores like sorting and filing. By the time I'd realized what happens when neither spouse is willing to perform unpleasant tasks, it was too late. We had to call in a recovery crew to help us find our tax records. Then we had to send in a search team to locate the recovery crew.

Among other marital surprises, I was shocked by how frequently that nasty "B" word surfaced. Every time my guy was angry he seemed to use it. That offensive noun kept rolling off his tongue. I hated it when he used the term "budget."

I'd managed to live for 35 years without that financial tool, so I saw little need to develop one now. Budgets only got in the way of my spending habits.

"Did we have that in our budget?" Jim would often ask.

"I don't know about yours," I'd reply, "but I just put it in mine."

Suffice it to say, philosophically, we differed.

Despite the hurdles we've encountered, we've been together now for nearly two decades, and neither of us has managed to change anything about the other. He's still averse to closing doors, relinquishing his recliner, and throwing away papers (even junk mail and flyers removed from the front door), and I continue to ignore housework, filing, and bank balances. I guess you could say we've compromised by agreeing to remain mutually annoyed.

Maybe we should have been wed on Thanksgiving.

Love Means Never Having to Say "Excuse Me"

While traveling on a book tour, Jim and I stopped to eat at one of our favorite Mexican restaurants: El Chaparral in Boerne, Texas. This began what we now simply refer to as "Bean-o-rama."

I'd forgotten that El Chaparral serves a small bowl of bean soup with each of its meals. Hubby and I had both ordered platters that further included refried black beans. By the time we returned to our hotel room, we were loaded with more than margaritas; we were packing major intestinal power.

As is our normal routine, we each planned to read before falling asleep. Curled up in bed together, Jim cracked open *The Secret*, a book about the power of positive thinking, while I entertained myself with a new novel. But only a chapter or two into our respective reading materials, our silence was punctuated with the interruption of familiar sounds—namely, flatulence.

Now, these were not the normal rooty-toot-toot kind of slips that occur during a momentary loss of manners. No. More like, full-scale, dirty-bomb, bring-in-the-hazmat-team-type emissions. It was a fart-fest of epic proportion.

Neither of us could seemingly control our gas or the associated laughter. The downside to this was that the more we cackled, the more we were forced to deeply inhale and the less we were able to maintain internal pressures.

After a fit of snorts and howls, Jim put down his metaphysical book and suddenly grew quiet.

"What?" I asked, fearing he'd suffered a stomach rupture.

"I'm practicing," he said real serious-like.

Probably he meant he was trying to use mind over physics. Maybe he thought he could hold his breath to rid himself of bloat, much the same way you supposedly can cure hiccups.

"Practicing what?" I pressed.

"My affirmations," he quipped. And then he began chanting, "My farts smell like Glade air freshener. My farts smell like Glade air freshener. My farts smell like ..."

"Well, it's not working," I snapped. "Not unless Glade makes a scent called 'Pinto Mist.'"

Now we were howling to the accompaniment of a full symphony of body sounds. If anyone had called room service, the poor delivery person would have likely keeled over before stepping 2 feet inside our doorway.

I looked into my man's eyes and, holding my nose, said, "You've got to be specific when you use thought to materialize what you want."

"You mean I need to state what scent instead of just saying 'air freshener'?" he asked. Right then, another foul-smeller cut loose, and he all but burst from his legume-induced hilarity.

"No," I replied, clutching my sides to keep from exploding. "I just realized that I should have been more careful when I asked to find my soul mate." I doubled over, now fully in stitches.

"What do you mean by that!"

Between hysterical fits of stop and starts, I managed to finally utter, "This wasn't what I'd had in mind when I asked for a man who'd *take my breath away*!"

Right then, we were both done in.

Sometimes romance is just in the air.

HOME & GARDEN

9-1-1

The Best Way to Clean a Garage

The four most terrifying words in the English language could be, "It's in the garage." Every time my spouse says this, I suffer chills, tremors, and potentially dangerous thoughts, such as, "Then neither of us will ever again find it, so I'll just purchase new lawn furniture."

Often hubby will look at me and say, "The next warm weekend that we're free, we need to tackle this garage." These declarations, though, aren't as fear-provoking as you might assume—because I know he'll never follow through on this threat.

My man is no more inclined to clean and organize the garage than I'm prone to rearrange our walk-in-if-you-dare pantry. You see, we share the theory that, when needed, important items will rise to the surface. And for anything that doesn't, there's always American Express.

Aside from the obvious risks of financial as well as personal injury, there are drawbacks to being this disorganized. For instance, I have to be careful when opening the automatic garage door. It's one thing to live this way, yet another to let neighbors witness it.

Generally, I whip inside the garage and, while the vehicle

continues edging forward, depress the button to close the metal curtain behind me. This action requires precision timing. If I don't calculate my entry just right, then the car doesn't line up like it should. But I've yet to run over anything of significant value.

I don't know how this storage area ever became so out of control. Our three-car garage barely houses one lawn mower.

In one corner we have a 4-foot-by-6-foot stack of bricks that the builders were kind enough to leave behind. I'm guessing they wanted us to have these extra materials in case an entire wall should ever collapse. Frankly, this made me a little skeptical about their building quality. However, I stopped worrying too much about the masonry after I learned that the crew also provided us with four cases of floor tiles and 27 leftover paint cans. For the record, I'd like to state that there's a fine line between thoughtfulness and laziness.

To these construction remains we've added a few offbeat collections of our own: empty computer cartons, three pairs of poison ivy-laced shoes, 14 tackle boxes (and we don't even fish), tiki torches that someone gave me so he could get them out of his own garage, weed killers that, as far as I know, won't work from the shelf where they've been stored for three summers, a hula hoop, a walking cane, the chainsaw that remains a risk to our health insurance provider, unusual colored rocks obtained from places I can't remember, and a turkey fryer that's been fired up only once—thanks to a nasty wind and grease incident.

Adding to this enclosure's ambiance are the potted plants that I've sheltered inside the garage during the winter. Now we have enough spiders residing out there to cast a film sequel to *Arachnophobia*. The last time I looked, the place had evolved into its own ecosystem.

For many, the problem with confronting a task of this magnitude is that they don't know where to begin. I, on the other hand, can identify the starting point. What I can't locate is the required energy.

The first step to cleaning out a garage is to simply pull out everything and set the contents on the driveway. Unfortunately, most communities now prohibit the second step. Therefore, I'm unsure what to suggest because it's unwise to violate burn bans.

So it looks like my garage may remain untouched for yet another season. But that's okay. It's never a good idea to tamper with an ecosystem.

Deedee's Rules for Picking the Perfect Patio Set

Every spring, I stare at the heap of lawn furniture in my backyard and wish I could make it disappear. I want to ditch the sun-bleached cushions and dirt-encrusted chairs, the cracked table top and mismatched umbrella, and buy a new patio ensemble. And each year, I come to the same conclusion: It doesn't matter what I purchase because, by next season, it'll look just like the set I have now.

I bet you have experienced similar frustrations. Here are a few tips to help you in your quest for the perfect outdoor furniture:

1. You MUST buy your patio set before May to obtain the best selection. After that, the mosquitoes arrive to remind people why it's hazardous to be outdoors. This, naturally, causes the stores to quit stocking inventory.

2. When shopping, if a salesperson greets you holding a

credit application (and especially if they mention an "EZ payment plan") then you'll want to look elsewhere for bargains.

3. Chair cushions are comfortable not only for humans but also nesting spiders, crumb-seeking ants, and leaf-born mold. Squirrels sometimes tear out and use cushion stuffing to insulate their nests. This proves these critters are intelligent enough to read labels containing words like "water resistant."

4. Tables come in two basic forms: the glass-top kind that's guaranteed to shatter, and the solid or wrought iron type that, if lifted, will give a healthy man a hernia. Pick your poison.

5. If you don't buy an umbrella, your guests will end up plugging the hole in the center of your patio table with an empty, upside-down beer bottle.

6. Unless you enjoy hoisting heavy metal chairs for sport, consider chaise lounges equipped with wheels. This provides the extra advantage of allowing you to use a chair, when needed, as a substitute wheelbarrow.

7. Invest in vinyl outdoor furniture covers. They won't keep your chairs clean, but they'll impress the heck out of your neighbors.

8. Color is important. White stays the coolest. Brown shows the least dirt. Chartreuse tells everyone that you have no class.

9. Don't waste your money on a bistro set. Everyone knows "bistro" is French for "overpriced and undersized."

10. Wood picnic tables attract wasps, aphids, and guests with small children. Sure, you can save a little money if you buy one. But is it really worth it?

Now, go take a gander at what's already sitting in your back yard. Looks pretty good, doesn't it?

Feng Shui for Closets

Whenever I'm restless and bored, I perform unnatural acts—like organizing closets. Generally, I get these urges once or twice a decade. A weird compulsion attracts me to the black hole that exists next to my master bathroom. I say "black hole" because entire ensembles have disappeared there. My daughter denies having ever borrowed any of my clothing, so I presume the heavy mass of coats, purses, shoes, and auto parts has simply folded in upon itself like a dense star.

Finally, I broke down and took an inventory of this closet. I discovered three boxes of items lost since 2002, a pair of hiking boots I purchased for a 1999 trip, and a mother-of-the-bride dress from a wedding that was cancelled the same year. All this before I'd made it past the bird clock, still in its original packaging, and an auto steering wheel. It was time to regain control of this space.

A quick study of Feng Shui, the Chinese art of placement, revealed how important it is for doors to swing freely open. Nothing should be stored behind a closet door, according to Feng Shui beliefs. Furthermore, nothing should be placed above the entrance because such practice produces feelings of depression and anxiety. Already I was experiencing those effects from simply looking past the door.

Feng Shui theory holds that closet clutter represents hidden problems impeding our progress in life, work, and relationships. Judging from the looks of my cache, I've been hampered by a disregard for time (bird clock), shortage of energy (hiking boots), and lack of a suitable vehicle (steering wheel) to achieve my goals.

I drew a deep breath, closed my eyes, and attempted to summon my chi.

Spaces that are completely full can block the flow of chi (vital energy), according to my Feng Shui guidelines. No wonder I'd been feeling lethargic lately. My walk-in closet had become a fashion freak house. I own more garment sizes than Kirstie Alley.

Avoid holding on to clothes until you've lost that 20 pounds, advised another article. What we let go of might benefit those in need, the writer suggested.

Examining my faded Dallas Cowboys Super Bowl shirt from 1996, I wondered who would want it.

The instructions I read stated that if I hadn't worn an item in the last two years, I'd probably never wear it again. Ha! If I haven't worn an article of clothing in the last two years, then it has likely been sitting in my laundry pile.

One expert suggested that I "avoid mixing my 'play' shirts with 'dress' blouses." But I couldn't see the point. After I did my wash, the tops would just get rearranged. Before I knew it, my good blouses would go right back to hanging out with some shirt from the wrong side of the rack.

To feel better, I peeked inside my husband's closet. However, I didn't walk into it for fear of radiation poisoning. His scuba gear, 14 duffle bags, a Dracula costume, three shoeshine kits, and enough baseball caps to outfit the entire

American League threatened to cave in on me. Appropriately, a fire extinguisher leaned against one wall.

"A full bedroom closet can block your ability to attract a new relationship," my Feng Shui instructions warned.

I shut the door to my man's private space and smirked. From the looks of it, I had extra marriage insurance. So that's one closet I won't be touching.

TAMING OF THE SHOE

Shopping for shoes has long been considered a woman's favorite pastime—right after hunting for men. In my case, the reason for this is simple. My feet are the only part of my anatomy that remains the same size despite how many French fries I've eaten. I can always find footwear that fits.

However, I've been careless about my shoe purchases. Not once have I stopped to contemplate what's in a style name. While my heels are well-suited to my wardrobe, they could be entirely wrong for my personality. And (gasp) what possibly could be worse than unknowingly wearing sandals called "Sweet Thing"?

Men, you too are at risk. Apparently, the tendency to identify footwear by alpha rather than numeric labels has infiltrated every department level. Consequently, women's, men's, teens' and even toddlers' shoes have been personified. It's no longer just a loafer you're looking for. It's a leathery likeness that's been cleverly named to match your individual taste.

Scanning recent sales brochures, I found a pair of men's sneakers titled "Rookie." Why would anyone want to be thought of as a beginner? Clearly, the better choice would be "Trouper" or maybe "Trammel," good, solid-sounding monikers.

"Jillian" seems to be a popular type of ladies' flats. I suppose Jillian is a likeable gal, but I'd have to seriously question the wedge heels whose namesake was "Drama."

OshKosh makes a version of toddler boys' sandals called "Gulfwind." When my sons were young, they wore Buster Brown shoes. I don't recall the styles, but one should have been named "Breakwind." Come to think of it, that title might be appropriate for a few men I know, too!

I wanted to find out how shoe style names were determined, me being a professional journalist and all, so I contacted Nine West, a shoe company, to find out. In an e-mail message I asked, "Do you have staff who sit around in a room and stare at a sandal and then unanimously decide that the shoe should be called 'Jester' or 'Daffodil?'"

I followed up my online communication with a voicemail message. Could there be both a 2005 "Odele" and a 2007 "Odele" for mature feet, I wondered. For all I knew, maybe the shoe-naming process was similar to designating hurricanes.

No corporate representatives responded to my inquiries. Probably the marketing folks were too busy trying to decide whether a sneaker had a sensible sole or expressive eyes.

Nevertheless, I decided to read the style names on a few of my husband's purchases to see what I might learn. In his closet I found a couple of shoeboxes, one of which said "Columbus." Looks like I've got an explorer on my hands, which is fine as long as he doesn't take his discovery urges too far. The next box read "Chocolat," which accurately describes his greatest addiction. And the last container was labeled "Air Moto Max," the suitability of which I believe I've already covered (see "Breakwind").

Apparently, without even knowing it, my guy had

purchased shoes that correctly revealed something about his nature.

In my own closet I uncovered a pair of boots named "Necessity" and some sandals called "Bartlett," which, as everyone knows, is a type of pear. I wouldn't make it through a winter without those boots, and I'm unquestionably pear-shaped, so either there was some kind of subliminal message at work or the universe has some perfectly weird laws of attraction.

The next carton I pulled from the shelf contained a label that read simply "Ellen." Does this mean I'll one day have my own TV show?

Do-it-Yourself Lawn Care

It's hard to live among do-it-yourself types when you're a get-somebody-else-to-fix-it person. "Do-it-yourself" turns up in my vocabulary only during conversations like this:

Husband: "I need this shirt ironed."

Me: "Do it yourself."

If I can't pay somebody soft wages for hard labor, then what's the point of owning a gym membership? I mean, other than bragging about a dedication to physical health despite never having actually visited any fitness facilities? However, I suppose membership alone has its rewards. I can truthfully answer yes if anyone ever asks—which, for some reason, no one ever does—whether I belong to a health club.

I avoid unpleasant tasks like workouts and yard duties because I'm allergic to sweating. Every time I perspire I develop a bad attitude. Thus, the only weekend warrior skills I possess are typically reserved for all-you-can-eat buffets.

Oh, sure, I'm missing the satisfaction of possessing a yard that could pass for a putting green. But the way I've got it figured, it's best not to tempt golfers. And anytime I want to enjoy the beauty of a lush lawn, all I have to do is open my door and stare out at my neighbors'. If I time it just right, I'm lucky enough to witness one of these grass-obsessed guys with his shirt removed. That's always a thrill. It's reassuring to know that I'm not the only one who avoids the gym.

My theory about people who devote entire weekends to working on their lawns is that they're the same ones who spend the least amount of leisure time at home. Don't get me wrong. I'm glad that they care so much about appearances. But I'd be equally happy observing these individuals doing something relaxing, like maybe sitting someplace prominent, chuckling and reading this book.

To me, all this fawning over landscapes seems silly. First, you have to rake all the dead leaves from your flowerbeds instead of letting nature turn them into dirt. Then, what's the very next thing you do? You head out to the nearest home and garden center to buy more soil!

At my house, the earliest signs of spring arrive in the form of weeds. I suppose this is so we can easily spot where to spray Roundup, that powerful deterrent that costs more per liquid ounce than holiday gasoline. I've no idea why my spouse is willing to pay so much for weed-killers when my son's dog can destroy any form of vegetation with death by urination. I could save a small fortune if only I could get the beast to go where he's instructed—or at least to develop better aim. I can't seem to get him to hit that spray bottle opening.

When I think of the money we spend on yard maintenance, regardless of who's providing the labor, I have to question why we bother. Who uses a front lawn, anyway? We probably wouldn't even have front yards if we weren't afraid of having our bedrooms crashed through by crazy drivers. So, in essence, we're throwing away our dollars to maintain a protective zone that has little probability of ever being used or visited by anyone other than toilet-papering hoodlums. (Note to toilet paper vandals: I'm just kidding. I didn't mean you.)

The only time my husband or I venture outside to the anterior of our lot is to retrieve the morning newspaper. Sometimes we'll stand there and he'll profess that it's time for someone to call our landscape crew. And fully agreeing with him, I'm the first to offer, "Why don't you do it yourself?"

Made Overseas, Broke in the U.S.

If consumers are the support beam of our economy, then shoddy merchandise must be the core foundation. Faulty products are, quite possibly, the top factor contributing to U.S. consumerism, followed by licensed character toys. However, I bring Batman into this discussion only for the express purpose of reaching a sufficient word count for this book.

From the looks of my household, companies no longer build items that are capable of lasting more than a few years. Today, you'll be lucky if an appliance is still operating when its zero-interest payments expire. Gone are the days of passing down a used refrigerator or washer and dryer to your children. Now you actually have to find another way to dispose of this equipment. That is, besides pushing it off into a ravine. Environmentalists have always frowned on that method, anyhow.

Nothing is built to last anymore. To prove this, everything I possess appears to be relocating itself from the asset to the liability side of my balance sheet—and I'm not just talking about my physical attributes.

My home air conditioner refuses to cool. My refrigerator's ice maker has broken, twice in one year. (They don't call it the "gold package" for nothing.) The 4-year-old automatic lawn sprinkler has sprung a leak that defies pinpointing. And both my car battery and alternator recently decided to expire at the same time—after just 50,000 miles and only a couple hundred episodes of leaving a passenger door ajar.

Naturally, my first thought was to search for a new home and vehicle. I mean, what kind of citizen would I be if I refused to burn cash on crummy replacement products? Why, that's no way to show my patriotism! That's no way to support the economy! Forget about saving and being frugal and purchasing quality items and hoping to one day maybe have a solid career from which I might retire. (Granted, maybe the "solid career" part was never a valid expectation.) For goodness sakes, this is America!

My washing machine decided to join the scrap heap when it began leaking worse than Paris Hilton's publicity camp. Like so many other appliances I'd owned, despite having the luster of a newly minted coin, this metal contraption had the shelf life of a banana.

One evening, while I was cleaning yet another washer spill (and practicing my command of expletives), I declared I'd had it with this sorry excuse for a laundry helper. "If one more thing around here breaks," I ranted, "I'm declaring consumer warfare!"

From his recliner, my husband craned his neck and asked, "Well, how old is it?"

"I don't know," I snapped. "We haven't had it that long. I think we bought it right after your dad died."

"It's probably time to replace it, then," he suggested, as if *The Antiques Road Show* should be consulted for an appraisal.

"It's already more than 5 years old."

Obviously he'd been brainwashed by The Machine—and I don't mean the washer.

"I'm tired of having to replace everything we own every three to five years," I huffed. "This is ridiculous. Maybe we should go back to scrub boards and pounding shirts on river rocks." Of course, I meant this only if he were going to assume the responsibility for doing laundry.

I swirled my mop in a circle, attempting to absorb the spill. "I'm getting nowhere, here," I whined.

Hubby appeared at the laundry room doorway. "All you're doing is making a bigger mess," he observed.

Studying the instrument in my hand, I suppressed the urge to swing it like a bat. "What else would you expect," I snapped, "from a mop that's nearly THREE years old!"

Appliance Overload

After my washing machine went kaput, I found myself inside a home improvement center, staring helplessly—which is the only way I ever appear inside one of these establishments.

Since I'd purchased my last laundry equipment seven years ago, washing machines had become more innovative. Once there'd been no more than a half dozen manufacturers' models—ranging from bachelor- to Brady Bunch-capacity levels—to choose from. No complex analysis had been required. Dryers came in two versions: electric or gas, which really didn't make much difference. Similar to a choice between being struck in the head with either a brick or a bowling ball, you could pretty much bet that, when it came to shelling out the dough for the utility bills, either one was likely to hurt you.

But suddenly I was faced with several rows of metal boxes to compare—some of which looked like they'd been snatched right out of a commercial Laundromat. The laundry room, that last bastion of simplicity, had been mucked up by someone who thought consumers needed more cleaning options. Here were machines in designer colors, washers and dryers equipped with tinted windows. I paused to consider the reasoning. Tinted windows? Does underwear require this much privacy?

I couldn't help but wonder. Do I really need to see what's going on inside laundry equipment? Sure, socks have a tendency to disappear in the wash, but who wants to monitor machines during laundry cycles? Given the chance, footwear will mate with sheet pockets regardless of who's watching.

Anyway, there I was, staring at one of those new-fangled top-loading washers, when a salesman approached. "These puppies are really something," he said, giving the unit a slap with his hand. Then he patted the matching dryer and added, "And this will steam clean your clothes so that they come out looking per-fect."

I glanced at the price tag that, I swear to Clorox, included a comma.

"This washer will spin your clothes so fast they'll need a lot less time to dry," the clerk said.

"Oh, I have my own method for that," I replied. "I normally forget the wash overnight. And by the next morning, the clothes are already half-dry!"

He gave me a puzzled look. "But these dryers are more energy efficient than the older models," he explained. "And there's this pedestal that you can put them on, too, so you don't have to bend over so far to load them."

"Hmm. I wonder why they didn't just make them the right

height to begin with?" I observed.

For several hundred dollars, I can now purchase all kinds of laundry room adornments, including pedestal bases, storage towers and special work surfaces. Though the way I've got it figured, when appliances start demanding to be accessorized, innovation has gone way too far.

"I'll take this pair," I said, pointing to a standard variety washing machine.

"Oh, these are more energy efficient than the older ones, also," said the salesman. "It's just that they're not as efficient as those over there." He motioned toward the equipment sporting the price tags with commas.

I felt bad for the guy. Maybe that's why I didn't bother to point out that the most energy-saving clothes dryer wasn't even in his department. It was on the rope aisle, and it sold for less than $20. In my parents' day, it was called a clothesline.

Dangerous Envelopes

We stood there, cautiously eyeing the envelope as though it might contain anthrax. "You open it," I said to my husband.

"No. You do it."

"How bad can it be? We've hardly been home for the past several weeks."

"Okay," he said, "I'll open it." He squeezed his eyes tight and counted. "One. Two. Three. One, two, three. One-two-three!" R-r-r-i-p.

The sealed threat now loosed, Hubby glanced down at the amount due and lapsed catatonic. I waived my hands in front of his face. No response. "Hon?"

The paper slipped from his hands and fell to the countertop. I lifted it and read, "Amount due: $697.67."

This couldn't be our electric bill!

Perhaps our cat had thrown wild parties while we were out of town. I glared at Miss Kitty. "Exactly how many friends do you have?" I scolded.

The meter reading had to have been wrong. "How often do you actually read these things?" I asked a company rep by phone. She said my power usage was audited hourly from an undisclosed location, sort of like the Nielsen TV ratings.

Apparently, my old electric monitoring device had been replaced with a "smart meter." And this high-tech gizmo is so intelligent that it's capable of outrunning every attempt I've made to slow it down. Clearly, it must not even stop for power outages.

I moved on to my next plan of attack. "How much have your rates gone up?" I huffed.

"Our rates haven't changed," said the customer service rep. "There's been an increase in the cost of natural gas to provide the power, and that power adjustment cost is passed straight through to the consumer."

I wasn't moving any closer to a lower bill.

No one should have electric fees the size of mine unless his or her last name is Rockefeller, Vanderbilt, or Cowell (as in Simon). This wasn't a utility charge. It was a substitute for a tropical vacation or holiday gifts for my entire family (minus me) or my spouse's wardrobe budget—for the next decade.

I checked my electric statement again, attempting to decipher the so-called "energy charge." In small print, nowhere near the amount due column, I found a string of numbers preceded by a decimal point (.0526210, to be exact). As best I could tell, after I've paid my bill, this is how much money I should have left over.

Next to the obscure percentage were either acronyms or words in Russian. I wasn't sure.

Later on, I discovered that PCRF stands for Power Cost Recovery Factor. This is the amount of extra money I have to pay the utility company to help offset their rising cost of natural gas. Well, how do I get a power cost recovery factor added to my wages? On second thought, that would price my work right out of the market—assuming there is a market for this stuff.

It seems I'll just have to make our home more energy efficient. Already I'm following most standard conservation advice. There's little left to do, short of tearing down the house and starting over with new construction—ideally the earth-sheltered kind.

Maybe I should replace all our exterior windows with Hardiplank. Or I could install one of those wind turbine generators in my backyard. Hey, it couldn't look any more unsightly than a cell tower.

I've got to do something because I can't afford to have utility bills that turn my mate into a mental zombie. (That battle already is being lost to televised sports.) And there's no way we can simultaneously pay for electricity and psychotherapy.

HEALTH, BEAUTY, & OTHER PRICEY PURSUITS

Final Impact

Right now, I can't be held accountable for what I write. It appears that I have water on the brain—and in my ears. When I speak, I sound like The Godfather. I know I'm not the only one who feels this way. Many people suffer sinus infections. However, the crud I'm battling might well be my "final impact."

It would be my luck to keel over after having written about a repulsive, nasal fluid that rhymes with "rot." When I first started writing, I swore I'd never imitate Dave Barry's booger humor. But I lied. I can't help it. When I'm drowning in my own body liquids, there's simply nothing else on my mind. Literally.

The worst part of this illness is that it not only makes me feel rotten but it also causes me to look stupid. I have become one of the very types I typically try to avoid—mouth-breathers. This means I can't chew with my lips closed and that I must sleep with my choppers wide open. But how can anyone rest knowing that a spider might crawl onto the bed, find a set of gaping jaws, and then embark on the next incredible journey? Consequently, I'm now also sleep-deprived.

"I read that some kind of pepper spray is supposed to

help dislodge this stuff," I said to my spouse. "But you can only find it online. And that's not going to help me tonight." Rummaging through our pantry, I discovered a jar of red pepper flakes. "Maybe this'll substitute."

I fumbled with the top and pulled free the plastic, perforated lid. The canister contained the aromas of ... well, I'd like to tell you, but I've lost my sense of smell.

Deeply, I inhaled.

Nothing happened.

"Maybe you ought to try sucking one of those flakes up your nose," my helpful hubby offered. "I bet that would do it."

"Right. If you really loved me, you'd try it first and tell me what it feels like," I snapped. And then I made a mental note to check whether he'd recently upped my life insurance.

Not long ago, I'd learned that chili powder can cause respiratory failure. Imagine what a nasal nodule full of pepper seeds might do. What had he been thinking?

To be honest, my soul mate and companion of 18 years would prefer that I recover. But if that's not going to happen within the next five minutes, he'd just as soon help me go faster.

Who can blame him, really? He's heard me clear my throat so many times that he's resorted to wearing his wireless headphones, even when the TV has been turned off.

"Hey, remember that thing we found in Mexico? That Mayan ear wax candle?" he asked.

"The one you stick in your ear and light to pull wax to the surface?"

"Yeah." He gave me a fiendish look and chuckled.

I recalled it well. When we discovered this tourist token, he asked me if it might work equally well for constipation, and we both collapsed with laughter. So I could see where our current conversation was heading. "No, I'm not going to stick one of those up my nose!"

It's nice to know my man cares this much about me when I'm sick. Nothing says "I love you" quite like a Mayan ear wax candle.

DNA: Dare to Ask?

A magazine article I read said the secret to my heritage lies in my blood. Well, actually, it resides in my cheeks. No, not those (although this has been debated). The ones on my face!

I can now trace my ancestry back to ancient times for less than the price of a professional portrait package. All that's required is a cheek swab sample.

For a fee between $100 and $200, a variety of genetic testing firms will generate a report of my DNA composition—one that attempts to identify my link to a symbolic Adam and Eve. From what I understand, no one has yet been traced back to the snake. But then again, to the best of my knowledge, my ex-husband hasn't been tested. Not that this would make any difference. I'm just saying ....

Findings from the National Geographic Society's Genographic Project reveal some interesting theories. If current DNA mapping project results are accurate, technically speaking, we all might be Africans—because that's where the genetic Adam and Eve originated.

Individuals who've had their DNA examined often learn their roots are attached to an unsuspected tree. For instance, genetic data suggest that Thomas Jefferson actively participated in a great deal more than politics. And according to a British DNA testing firm, the Ice Man (that 5,300 year-old frozen corpse found in the Italian Alps) apparently had relatives who got around even more than he did.

I've been thinking maybe I ought to have my own DNA test conducted. It's possible that I'm not really a mix of Scot, Irish, Welsh, and German, like I've been told. What if I'm a descendant of some obscure indigenous tribe that harbors a recessive trait for clumsy sentence structures and droll humor? Good grief. My entire self-image could be altered overnight.

Once my genetic test results have been prepared, I can choose to enter the findings into a database to help me find hundreds, if not thousands, of living relatives previously unknown. But why would I want to do that? I mean, that would only create an equal number of chances that these folks might contact me to borrow money. My holiday gift list is already long enough.

Given my luck, I'd probably discover I'm related to Lucy—the missing link, not the comedian. I saw this prehistoric woman's bones once at the Smithsonian Museum, and I have to tell you that she looked a whole lot more ape than human.

Speaking of apes, what if I found out I was kin to someone like Attila the Hun? Then I'd have no defensive argument to offer the next time my husband accused me of this.

Still, there could be advantages to participating in genetic testing. I could prove, once and for all, that I'm not an alien from the planet Weirdtune—and put an end to any further speculation about my sense of rhythm. Who knows what deep mysteries might be uncovered and resolved?

Possibly, I have distinguished relatives I've never met. Why, for all I know, Oprah and I could be cousins. That's the kind of information I'd deem worthy of a cheek swab. To obtain this beneficial data, I might even consider ingesting the collector stick!

GENETICALLY IMPROBABLE HAIR

My greatest physical challenge can be summed up in two words: wild hair.

Women's magazines endlessly feature styles that work best for different hair types. The articles typically say something like, "These are perfect cuts for those with fine, limp hair," or "If your hair is wavy, try this look." Well, I have coarse, wavy, and thick locks. When I turn to the page that shows which styles work best for hair like mine, all I ever find is a single photo—of a bald woman.

When I travel, I feel sorry for the people who occupy hotel rooms next to mine, especially if I have to rise at 3 a.m. to catch an early flight. I'm not one of those people who can simply whip my hair into a ponytail and go. No way. This sometimes causes me to operate a blow dryer in the middle of the night for about a half hour, until the circuit breaker flips or the appliance motor shorts out, whichever occurs first.

At home, I don't bother with hair dryers—a turbo-charged leaf blower works better—but those are difficult to pack inside a carry-on.

My mother's hair is a lot like mine, only hers receives fewer invitations to participate in mutation studies.

Frankly, I think Mom's dietary habits might be more to blame than genetics. There's an old wives' tale that suggests what a woman eats during pregnancy can affect her unborn child. I'm thinking maybe Mom had a love affair with kiwi fruit during my gestation. And she must have eaten the skins.

Why do some people have hair like silk, and yet mine looks more like something DuPont should consider as a replacement for Olefin?

To make matters worse, according to fashion magazines, I have a diamond-shaped face. That's a nice way of calling me a "pointy head."

Not just any hairstyle will complement my features. In fact, the choices are extremely limited. When you look under "suitable styles for diamond-shaped faces," there should be an asterisk, followed by the words, "for those unable to afford reconstructive surgery."

Stylists will do everything in their power to drive me away. One guy who did my hair for 10 years finally gave up. He moved without leaving me his forwarding address or telephone number. My next stylist was conveniently on vacation every time I needed her services.

My current hairdresser keeps trying to convince me I can change the texture of my hair by simply using more expensive products. After applying some of these conditioners to the challenge, she directed my hands to the back of my head and said, "Feel your hair!" I touched the newly softened layers. Then she remarked, "It feels like" —she appeared to be searching for words—"like *normal* hair," she exclaimed.

Someone else might have been offended, but not me. I was just elated that she hadn't yet skipped town.

Needless Needles

Occasionally people ask me (mostly when they're drunk or wanting to borrow money) why I never aspired to become a screen star. To be honest, I'm an ill-suited candidate because, in addition to my average appearance and love affair with carbohydrates, I'm encumbered by a terror of needles. All the body and facial enhancements required to maintain a youthful look for today's film industry are out of the question for me.

Botox? Uh-uh, no way! Lipo-suction? Have you seen the wand that surgeons use to liquefy and extract human lard? Why, I'd rather run a marathon a month than undergo that kind of violation. And the only way I'm getting a face lift is if my husband tilts my chin up.

I've been afraid of needles ever since fourth grade. That's when I was herded into a group and branded by my first TB test and initial brush with death.

In small groups, students lined up in front of a nurse who gave each child a quick tap on his or her inner wrist with a pen-like metal instrument. The stamp left a dime-size ring of pin pricks that didn't hurt much but caused a fractional amount of bleeding.

When my clan returned to our homeroom, the next batch of students filed out. Any remaining fourth-graders whose time had not yet come rushed over to see what had happened to those recovering from the procedure. I remember a boy looking over my shoulder and shrieking, "You're blee-ee-ding!" And, indeed, on my skin surface set a freckle-sized bead of scarlet.

Though I wasn't conscious during the next part of this story, I believe the events unfolded something like this: Fainting at the thought of my escaping life force, I fell out of my student-size, plastic-molded chair and cracked my noggin on the tile flooring. This caused my eyes to roll back into my head, like a zombie's, and my lids to jerk partially open.

I can't say where my consciousness might have traveled, but my hearing remained right there in that room. My sympathizers' remarks were audible, yet I couldn't respond to them.

"SHE-E-E-E'S DEAD!" one of the children screeched. And that instigated a surge of screams.

"I'm not dead," I wanted to say. But my mouth wouldn't work. The more the kids screamed and hollered, however, the more I wondered if maybe I had checked out. After all, I had no idea what death was or how it might feel.

"Look at her EY-EY-EY-ES!" a girl yelled. "They're O-O-O-PEN!"

"EE-EE-EE-CH! AH-AH-AH-AH!" the group cried in unison.

Next, I heard footsteps and the sounds of grownups returning to chaos. I'm guessing the TB test line had grown significantly shorter right about then, because my fellow compadres had launched a full revolt. With one kid down, nobody intended to volunteer to become the next premature death.

"Children, please stop hollering," my teacher commanded. "Step back! Diana is NOT dead. She's simply fainted."

Then the school nurse assaulted me with a vial of smelling salts (which was a far cry from nurturing, if you ask me). I blinked hard and tried to focus on the ceiling. From my horizontal position, I could see dozens of frightened faces peering down at me.

"She's AAAA-LIIIIVE!" somebody yelled. And then everyone applauded.

I glanced at my feet, which remained splayed in my chair. To my horror, I noticed my dress was open like an umbrella, exposing all my goods to full view.

You could say that was sufficient stardom for me. Ever since that day, I've had no desire to become a threat to Sharon Stone.

How to Look 10 Pounds Thinner in a Swimsuit

Near-biblical levels of rain in North Texas have produced some positive upsides. Our lakes are once again full. And, thanks to the downpours, there have been few swim parties.

Don't get me wrong. I love a fun poolside event. I just hate to be seen half-naked by people who once thought I was of normal size (if not intelligence) because previously all they'd witnessed of me was my doctored up headshot in the newspaper.

When I receive an invitation to a pool party, I figure someone who's either younger or less averse to cardio fitness is trying to shame me into shaping up. Perhaps if I could stare at my toes and in the process see everything between my abdomen and my ankles, I'd feel different. But it's unlikely that I'll ever find out.

Like many, I vowed to lose 15 pounds before swimsuit season. Unfortunately, it was the 1992 season. And I'm still working on it.

So naturally I was intrigued by a caption from an online article that promised solutions to help me "look 10 pounds thinner in a swimsuit." However, when I clicked on the link and read the advice, I couldn't help but scoff. One of the methods mentioned was, I'm not kidding, "sit up straight." How, exactly, will stretching my spine make my thighs look trimmer?

Because my mind works the way it does (which can best be described as intermittently), I came up with a few more tips for how to look thinner in a swimsuit this summer. And since I'm always willing to share ideas, here's the list:

Ways to look 10 lbs. thinner this swim season

1. Always stand. Never sit. (Standing keeps thighs from lapping over lawn chairs.)

2. Don't go underwater where everything appears 20% bigger than it really is, unless you're a man and somehow that sounds beneficial.

3. Never hold your breath because hot air expands.

4. Contour your widest body parts by painting them with a darker shade of self-tanner.

5. Wear platform flip-flops to make yourself appear taller. You'll still look overweight, but at least now you'll seem statuesque and full-figured instead of just short and dumpy.

6. Slather your stomach with Preparation H.

7. To hide upper arm flab, wear your child's water wings.

8. Suck in your belly and walk backward.

9. Buy a suit that includes an attached, calf-length swim skirt.

10. Wear swimwear made of camouflage print. If you don't look thinner, at least you'll blend in with the landscape.

Despite this advice, I remain reluctant to be seen in my bathing suit. Thus, I continued my surfing online. That's when I saw the eBay listing for a Miraclesuit. A miracle? Yes, yes! That's exactly what I was looking for! I needed a garment that would make me appear as svelte as a gazelle.

"Look four sizes smaller," the teaser said. Notice the lack of reference to "dress" sizes or "pants" sizes in that suggestion. Possibly the seller meant tablecloth sizes.

Another mouse click led me to the complete description and image of this magical maillot. When the picture came into view, I carefully studied the black swimsuit adorn with three, horizontal white stripes. I couldn't believe it. An identical one was hanging in my closet!

There's nothing more demoralizing than searching for a beauty miracle that's already been received. Now I'm deeply depressed because I'm not just overweight. Evidently, when I put on my swimsuit, I'm four sizes larger than I appear! I sure hope that's not four tablecloth sizes.

Fair Warning

A few months after I met my future husband, Jim, he gave me a puzzled look and asked, "Why would anyone want to go to the state fair?" He's originally from Ohio, where fair attractions include toy train displays, plaster exhibits, and the world's largest work boot, so I could understand his inquest. His parents had never introduced him to the positive germ resistance benefits of children's barnyards. And the closest thing he'd ever seen to a pig race had been one sausage truck trying to pass another on the Interstate.

All state fairs aren't created equal. My spouse has come to appreciate this during our marriage. At some fairs you can buy cotton candy, household products, and trinkets. However, at the State Fair of Texas, you can obtain considerably more than car wax, stainless cookware, and other seldom used products. There's also exquisite handcrafted jewelry! One year, when Jim was working out of town, I had the pleasure (and available line of credit) to take home an heirloom state fair souvenir.

For those who might be debating reasons to attend local festivals, here are some universal attributes you may want to consider:

Deedee's reasons to attend a fair

- To have your walking exercise rewarded every 20 feet by a different food group.
- To witness how enormous and obese swine can get if they're not made into pork chops.
- To brush bodies with strangers without the threat of being arrested.
- To escape household cleaning or yard work.
- To test your skills (find parking), endurance (restroom lines), and dental work (candy apples).
- To feel the freedom of beverage vendors who won't keep tabs on the number of beers you drink.
- To lose your spouse in the crowds.
- To see this many thrill seekers performing such an assortment of stupid, life-threatening acts in one place.
- To daringly sample fatty foods that could be classified as "deadly weapons"—deep-fried avocados, battered and fried cheesecake on a stick, and fried PB&J sandwiches, to name a few.
- To compare your personal talents to those displayed in the arts and craft pavilions, which may justify weeks of self-loathing.

- To let men experience real-life examples of flashy cars attracting beautiful, busty women. The guys don't need to know that these "hotties" have been paid to stand there and talk to them.

- To test your aim and wit against a carnie with an eighth-grade education who, in all probability, will get the last laugh when he empties your pockets.

- To have more family fun than possible anywhere else—short of spending your day with an overgrown mouse.

I like to visit the State Fair of Texas with my children and grandchildren. This year, they announced they're planning to see Big Tex on a weekday. "I'm going to the fair with the kids on Wednesday," I said to hubby.

Without hesitation, he replied, "Then I'll be taking off work."

Apparently, he's come to see the advantages in participating.

NEVER WEAR A FANNY PACK—ESPECIALLY NOT TO A STATE FAIR

My son and daughter-in-law gave me a calendar to help me remember important dates like their birthdays. However, one of the photos inside caused me to demolish a bedroom.

The 8 x 10 pictures of my grandchildren were a joyful reminder of family. But when I flipped to the month of October, I found a rotund woman revealing her dimpled, bare arms and a turkey wattle neck, impersonating me!

In disbelief I stared at the picture of the lady wearing a

familiar-looking outfit and fanny pack. She appeared to have been standing inside the State Fair of Texas next to my two grandkids.

I remembered that day because I had been there, and I'd eaten half my body weight in funnel cakes, corn dogs, and Dippin' Dots before I'd even found the main food pavilion.

Permit me to digress and say that nobody should ever wear a fanny pack. You might just as well swallow your camera, car keys, and eye glasses—because when you cram all those items into your zippered carrier it's going to appear that you did, indeed, eat them. Either this or that you are harboring some kind of aggressive stomach tumor.

Witnessing this hideous image, I immediately declared that it wasn't me. Then I burned those baggy Capri pants that I'd been wearing so no one could ever prove differently. And as a painful last resort, I vowed to lose weight.

As anyone knows, there are only two ways to shed pounds: eat less or cut your hair. My hair is already short, so the latter option wasn't available. Instead, I carried the last of my high-calorie treats to a friend's party. My banana nut bread was given to a hostess who owns one of those vibrating workout benches—so she deserved whatever she was left with.

The next day, I started an exercise program that included spending time on the treadmill that I'd uncovered while putting away laundry.

I decided to watch television to help distract me from my mind-numbing walk. Straddling the equipment, I tuned to the Food Network channel.

Soon my muscles cramped, my head felt light, and my body was drenched with either sweat or saliva; I couldn't be sure which because I was watching a cooking program.

Probably my speed had been too fast. Checking, I

discovered the treadmill was set on "cool down."

I was determined to go the distance despite my pace. Exhausted and gulping air, I glanced at the clock to see how much time had elapsed.

Three minutes.

Another 27 minutes of lighter impact exercise—possibly speed typing—would be necessary. So I decided to change my king-size mattress pad, which always provides an excellent cardio workout.

I completed another 5,000 steps by simply trying to connect the upper corners of the cover to the mattress. Every time I tugged on the top right corner, the far left one would pop off.

Finally I pumped on the third fitted cavity, which required at least 100 pounds of torque to fasten down. Latched in place on three sides, the mattress pad's fourth and final pocket remained. Red-faced and well on my way to a date with Preparation H, I bent my knees and yanked and pulled, turning myself into a human winch.

Right then, the upper left corner cut loose.

Like an errant sling-shot, the mattress cover fired across the bedroom, wiping out two framed photos, a clock radio, and the last of my desire for exercise.

It seems I'm simply not cut out to be a calendar girl.

In Case of Emergency, Break TV Screen

If I'm ever seriously ill, I hope someone will take me to the hospital where the TV series *House* is filmed. Probably, there are no other medical facilities where doctors struggle as hard as these actors do to diagnose obnoxious patients. I know because I'm one of those difficult clients.

Right off, when I enter a doctor's office, I display attitude. Part of my problem is that I think a majority of physicians are drug pushers. If you're a man, you may go to see a doctor because you've broken an arm or leg and leave with samples of Viagra. To many wives, by the way, this is not a perceived benefit.

If you're female, you might complain of weight gain and receive a prescription for hormone replacement therapy, laser hair removal, and support hose, even if you had only one chin whisker.

One of my doctors keeps insisting that, in addition to my prescription meds, I should to be taking calcium. Recently, she reiterated this instruction.

"I can't," I whined. "It doesn't digest well."

"What do you mean by that?" she asked.

"Well, broccoli is a high source of calcium. Right?"

"Correct."

"Okay, that's what I mean. Every time I eat it, I get gas."

"You can get it in pill form," she insisted.

Now I ask you, who would want to take broccoli pills?

I don't know why we were even talking about vegetables because I'd been trying to describe to her a tingling feeling I'd been experiencing. "But what about all these weird sensations I'm having?" I asked. "What do you think is the cause?"

Like a coward, she referred me to a neurologist.

Television medical staff all scramble around with their faces screwed up, consulting with each other about symptoms and rare disorders—and they don't stop researching until they have an explanation for what ails their patients. Within less than 30 minutes they conclude something astounding like, "Her belly is filled with a 29-foot tapeworm!"

But in real life, to get discovered that sucker would've had to have leapt out of the patient's mouth and assaulted the practitioner with his or her own tongue depressor.

I visited a neurologist, and my temperament only worsened. After I'd chronicled my history of numbness, tingling, chronic pins and needle-like pains, he instructed me to remove my shoes and socks. Then this wise medical healer leaned in close, slipped a diagnostic tool (otherwise known as a sharp metal spike) from his jacket pocket, and stabbed me in the end of one big toe. "Can you feel this?" he asked as if I might be paraplegic.

A scene from the movie *Dirty Rotten Scoundrels* flashed before my eyes—the one where Steve Martin's character's thighs are bludgeoned to prove he's been faking a disability.

I jumped about two feet into the air, tears pooling in the moon slits of my eyes, and sucked in a breath that seemingly couldn't be exhaled. And then, when I was able to again project sound, I howled so loudly that the blare caused nearby residents to seek out storm shelter.

The only possible explanation I can provide for this brutal behavior (the doctor's, not mine) is that the neurologist must have been trying to discern whether I could tell the difference between an imaginary pin prick sensation and the real deal. I left him with a clear understanding that I could. (He's expected to eventually regain normal hearing.)

On the bright side, at least I don't have a 29-foot tapeworm.

The Cure for SAD

Having made a dramatic entrance into the house from the garage, I caught my husband's attention. "The doctor said I'm a SAD victim," I announced, collapsing onto the sofa. "You better make dinner. I'm feeling too weak."

"What the heck is that supposed to mean?" he asked.

"It means I need more sunlight and possibly a second home in the tropics." I gazed at the burnt out ceiling lights overhead and sighed. "I'm suffering from Seasonal Affective Disorder."

I should have suspected something was wrong when in September I started sleeping until 8 a.m. Soon after, I began consuming only truffles and chips for lunch. By October I'd gained five pounds and didn't want to see another soul until I'd lost this weight. A full breakdown occurred in November. When no one else was home, I finished off the last of our leftover Halloween candy. After that, I couldn't even face the Christmas cookies. It was too depressing.

Earlier, my physician had suggested remedies to help me get through this periodic phase of binge eating and withdrawal. "You really ought to try and get plenty of sunshine and rest," she said, recalling my cyclical behaviors. Every year, starting in fall and continuing into early summer, I offer her the same tired complaints: increased drowsiness, constant hunger, and bouts of lethargy and depression.

If only I could escape to a more temperate climate and snare some serious solar contact, I might feel better. I longed to savor sunshine brilliant enough to make me squint, and I didn't have time to wait for spring's eventual arrival. At the rate my symptoms were progressing, by then I'd have accumulated too much heft to move.

"I have an idea!" I replied. "Why don't you write me a prescription for a 10-day cruise? Do you think you could convince my insurance company to pay for that?" Given the way my last claim had been processed, I should have known better. For some reason, my medical coverage provider hadn't agreed that spa treatments were necessary to cure a sinus infection.

The doctor appeared stoic. She studied my sallow complexion and drooping shoulders. "You may be feeling the effects of too much melatonin," she advised.

"I doubt that. It's been months since I've been able to tan."

She gave me a quizzical look. "I believe you've confused melatonin with melanin."

I wanted to say, "Oh, yeah? Well that's why you're still paying for your education and I'm not!" But I just smiled and shook my head. "Either way, I could use the excursion."

According to mental health experts, SAD affects women more often than men, so I really didn't expect my husband to understand. He thinks getting out of bed every morning before sunrise is a wholly natural act—and I'm certain there's no surer way to cause daytime fatigue.

"I think you're overreacting," Hubby suggested when I tried to explain. "That sounds like a bogus term to me."

"Easy for you to say," I huffed. "You're not the one who's

got a weakened immune system and several more months of darkness threatening to kill you."

From what I've been told, my symptoms might improve if I take medication, spend more time outdoors, or linger longer over fine jewelry counters. Full spectrum light, the kind you get from sunshine and certain artificial sources, is the recommended antidote for SAD.

One medical Web site I checked suggested that, for a few hours each day, I place myself underneath a bunch of those plant "grow lights." But what if they made my hips bloom?

No. If I'm expected to make a full recovery anytime soon, I'm going to need a Caribbean vacation. That's simply all there is to it. Otherwise, my circadian rhythms are going to be too out-of-whack for me to think crooked. And nobody wants that.

Those who wish to render aid, please feel free to do so. You may send your fully taxable contributions in the form of cash, checks, or cruise line gift certificates to Deedee's SAD Fund. I'll graciously accept airline miles, too. I promise to mention all donors in a future book, and each contributor will receive an original, autographed postcard from an as-yet-to-be-determined tropical locale.

If I raise enough money, I might even venture as far as Australia—because it's summer there when it's winter here in the United States.

"Ahoy!" I say. It's time for SAD sufferers to unite. We need no longer remain hidden, craving carbs and fingering our deserts in the dark. Warmer climates and sunnier days are but a cruise away. Together, we can fight the effects of this debilitating disorder.

Now, if you'll excuse me, I need to dim the wattage on this plant light. I'm afraid my thighs are on the verge of blossoming!

LOONEY
LEISURE

Riding in Cars with Kids

Many will attempt to conquer the great American challenge—the family road trip. Oblivious to the pending dangers, these adventurers will set out to find the much sought after and ever illusive "family fun" activity only to discover there's no such thing. This is a fantasy created by entertainment companies like Disney. You can have personal fun, dating fun, couple's fun, but you can never, ever, reach the pinnacle of bliss—the point where every member of your extended entourage is equally happy.

If you are traveling with a teen, you will in all likelihood learn that, on the evening before your trip, he or she has broken up with a recent girlfriend or boyfriend. Unfortunately, you will discover the reason for your youngster's surly attitude only after you've been home for a few weeks and have received your bill for 3,000 minutes of text messaging.

The discontentment begins within 200 miles of home, exactly where you can expect to run out of range of popular radio stations. After this, unless you have satellite radio or CDs on hand, your song choices will be limited to two types: country tunes and western music. This will cause the aforementioned puberty-afflicted to become irritable and to start thumping the back of his or her sibling's head, which will then naturally produce the automated response, "M-o-o-m-m, make him stop hitting me!"

Smart parents will provide for a "no touch zone" between all underage passengers. Do not try to artificially create barricades for offspring by inserting cargo between them. This will only result in lost merchandise. And never give a child your pillow to use for a headrest because car trips have a hypnotic effect on small children, causing them to drool worse than a Saint Bernard.

Always be sure that the total headcount does not exceed the number of auto interior cup holders. Otherwise, you will most assuredly be left holding a soda can for 2,000 miles.

Expect to synchronize meals but never bladder functions. Everyone will want to eat at once, but you can bet each person will ask to whiz only when nobody else has to.

By the time you've stopped for gas, disembarked for each urgent body function, and taken breaks for sustenance, you can expect your speed to average about 35 miles per hour and your gas mileage to hover around 10 miles per gallon. Oh, sure, the new car sticker might have suggested your vehicle would get 30 mpg on the highway. But that figure didn't take into account the wind drag from the bike rack addition and the 600 extra pounds of beverages, sporting gear, and sneakers you loaded into the transport before leaving home.

Fatigued navigators will be further aggravated by the posterior assault visited upon them by any young ones situated behind the driver's seat. And the opposite parent will either blatantly disregard his or her duties or simply be too weary to supply necessary travel directions. This will become obvious approximately 20 linear feet prior to a spaghetti-like interchange.

If you are prone to fairness, get over it. Now is not the time to be democratic about critical decisions, such as where to stop for lunch. Ignore this piece of advice and you will find yourself dropping by a Starbucks right before visiting Randy's Roadhouse Billiards & Brisket, followed by trips through the drive-thru lanes of both KFC and McDonald's.

Remember: Your goal, should you decide to accept the road trip challenge, is to simply create memories and return home with all parties speaking to each other. At the very least, by the second week.

AMERICAN VACATION

Our Disney World trip had been planned for several months when my husband unexpectedly lost his job. "We have to cancel," Jim declared. "Now is not the time to take an expensive vacation." Being my usual self, I showed my mature side. Okay, maybe I behaved a bit childishly. All right, I threw a fit.

"Years from now, the kids will remember this trip as the pinnacle of their young lives," I said. "No amount of money could possibly be worth depriving them of seeing Mickey and Minnie, Chip and Dale, Cinderella and—" I clutched my chest "—Prince Charming." I didn't explain that my own parents had never taken me to Disney World and that this trip meant more to me than it did to our offspring.

So we loaded up the minivan, tossed three children (ages 6, 14, and 15) into the vehicle, and set out on an interstate journey that carried us 3,000 miles closer to insanity.

Our first fiasco occurred before we'd made it past the Dallas city limits.

"What's that noise?" I asked.

"I don't hear anything," said Jim. "You're always

imagining things. Why don't you relax? Everything's under control."

He was right, I told myself. I'm ridiculously hyper-vigilant when we travel.

The faint flapping sounds I'd heard earlier disappeared and then, a few seconds later, returned. I recalled the suitcases we'd strapped to the overhead luggage rack. "Did you tie those bags tight?" I pressed. "Are you sure they're not coming loose?"

One of the teens sighed.

"I secured them with bungee cords," Jim reassured. "Now will you quit worrying?"

No sooner had he said this than we all heard an ominous whop-whop-whop, and then a thump. I spun to look out the rear window only to observe our suitcases tumbling, one by one, end over end, down the middle of LBJ Freeway.

After we'd brought our van to a halt, I watched in horror as cars clipped and dodged the runaway luggage. Before I could yell "Stop!" hero hubby bounded into the roadway to reclaim our belongings.

Right then, all I could think was, "Do we still have insurance coverage?"

Nobody got hurt. However, our tweed suitcase suffered a nasty road rash that left its innards exposed.

We arrived at Disney World on day two. There, we discovered that our crew lacked the crucial ability to compromise. Our youngest wanted to see the castle and hang out with Chip and Dale and Goofy, while the teens would just as soon have been observed holding each other's hands. (And believe me, the only physical contact these two ever displayed occurred during combat.)

On our final day of Disney, we left earlier than planned.

The children had engaged in a brawl that spilt over to the remaining family members. Having lost his patience, our reluctant leader left the rest of us seated in the van while he paced the gargantuan parking lot. When he'd had enough of the 98-degree temperatures, he returned to his seething kin.

"Just take me to the airport," I said. "I'll catch a plane home. This bunch is all yours. I can't endure another second of this bickering." Of course, I wouldn't have followed through on that threat. My endurance for family friction had simply run out.

From the back of the van came a small voice. "Can I just say something, here?" asked my 6-year-old. He'd been relatively quiet through the relentless arguments about which rides to choose and what foods to eat.

"Sure. Why not? What do you want to say?" I replied.

"I wanted to say that I love y'all all very much," he said softly.

Tears flowed. Children and parents hugged. The van started, and we completed our vacation without further incident. Sometimes a declaration of love is all that's required to save us from destruction.

Today, all our children are grown. Already, I've made the trip back to Disney World with one of them—and two of my grandchildren. My husband even agreed to join me for that sequel. You see, we both believe family vacations are important because they have a way of teaching us to better appreciate home and one another.

During my first trip to Disney World, I learned it wasn't necessary to travel 3,000 miles to see Prince Charming. He's never been that far away. He's the man who risked his life to save my luggage. And he's the guy who has, on several occasions, sacrificed his sanity for the sake of a child's happiness.

Ridiculous Road Signs

Some of the topics that tickle my brain—okay, practically all of them—could be considered mundane by those who possess any literary standards. However, since you're reading this, it's fair to assume that you're not among that group.

Take road signs, for instance. (Please don't actually "take" them because that's against the law.) Most people never think about them one way or the other. But I'm amused by the cryptic information and warnings that traffic signs convey. So, one day, I asked my husband, "Don't you think it's funny when you see a sign that says something like 'Guard Rail Damage Ahead'? I mean, what are we supposed to do? Turn back because there's no guard rail?"

Steering our vehicle into a tight curve, my devoted protector replied, "I don't know. I never notice signs."

Ever since we had that conversation I've been more frequently asserting myself for driver duty. And as a result, I've observed even more road warnings with comical implications. Here's a short list:

Watch for Falling Rock – If I drive with my eyes turned heavenward, how can I see where I'm going?

Yield to Ramp – I've never witnessed a ramp move, so how can I yield to one?

Stop When Flashing – Flashers who stop generally get caught!

Right Lane Must Exit – Yes, the lane will exit. But the cars in it can be expected to do just about anything, and that's what drivers most need to notice.

Freeway Ends – And your point is ...? Because I intend to keep going.

Historical Marker Ahead – Why do we need a marker to announce a marker?

Prepare to Stop – What must one do to prepare? Test the brakes? Lock the doors? How much planning is required?

Shoulder Work Ahead – You shouldn't be driving on the shoulder of the road, anyway!

Construction Zone – This should read, "No workers for the next 10 miles."

Uneven Lanes – Who are they kidding? You will flip your automobile if you change lanes in one of these areas!

SLOW (handheld sign displayed by worker) – We already know the speed at which these crews work. Do we really need to ostracize one guy for being less expedient than the rest?

Left Lane for Passing Only – Most drivers interpret this to include passing time.

Drive Slow. We Love Our Children. – As opposed to what? Extra points for taking out pedestrians?

Obey Traffic Signs – Isn't this kind of like telling your kids, "I'm giving you an order to obey my orders?"

Of course, to read a traffic sign with any seriousness you must first see it. That immediately eliminates my mate. He could not only fail to recognize the peripheral object, but he might also misunderstand its instructions.

While on vacation in Arizona, our family encountered a lone woman standing in the desert and holding a full-size stop sign, pole and all. No other vehicles were anywhere within sight. My guy rolled our vehicle to a halt and then, mindlessly, as though he'd just obeyed a residential traffic sign, continued to move forward.

The lady sporting a bright orange vest frantically waved her arms in the air, causing hubby to brake hard again. Dragging her metal sidekick by its neck, she sauntered over to the driver's side window and, as my spouse lowered the glass, leaned in close. "I *am* holding a *stop* sign, here," she admonished.

Without missing a beat, my daydreamer replied, "Uh-huh. And I stopped!"

In the back seat my 13-year-old son had doubled over. The two of us were in a race to see who might wet their shorts first. But the gal attached to the movable signpost never cracked a smile. Right then, I considered it fortunate that she was unarmed. Otherwise, she might have shot us for failure to yield to authority.

Pay attention. Read the signs. And never, ever question a woman who's overheated and underpaid.

Why Women Won't Read Maps

Often men depend on women to provide driving directions, though I can't imagine why. Girls are not born equipped with "you are here" indicators. However, I admit this would be advantageous during certain interactions with the opposite sex.

From what I can tell, there are only two kinds of female navigators: those who can't read a map and those who can but prefer not to.

One explanation for why women balk at roadmaps can be found by looking at an automobile's structural design. The front passenger seat area offers the implied freedom of mindless travel. Otherwise, this section would include a second brake pedal rather than a glove compartment and lighted visor mirror.

Despite my reputation for misguidance, my husband steers the car while I stare at a map and pretend to know exactly where we are when we're on vacation.

Helpfully, my man will call out streets as he notices them. "That was Church Street we just passed," he'll say. And I'll place a finger squarely on "Conch Street" and mumble something affirmative.

"Are we on North or South Ocean Drive?" he'll ask. And I'll answer that we are most definitely on one or the other.

Reading a map is actually quite easy—once I've found my eyeglasses. It's the comprehension part that gives me trouble.

Cartographers seldom note critical landmarks, such as malls, supermarkets, and ATM kiosks. Furthermore, mapmakers provide something called a directional key and a mileage scale that I find useless. Such tools could be beneficial only to someone who travels with a compass and a ruler.

To make things even more difficult, map producers sell ad space to businesses. So I typically end up directing us to some place like Island Gemstones instead of the botanical gardens. Hey, flowers are temporary. Tanzanite is forever.

While touring Grand Cayman Island, I managed to get us turned around several times. "Now what?" asked my demanding chauffeur. He'd just encountered a forced turn. "Do I go left or right?"

"I don't know. Just drive towards the coastline," I instructed.

Hubby looked at me straight-faced and replied, "We're on an *island*. There's a coastline in every direction."

Some people will go to any length to "one-up" you.

The roundabouts had confused me. Signage at these traffic circles is posted only a few feet before the entry points. By the time I'd realized we were approaching a roundabout, it was too late to check which way to go.

Fortunately, these vehicular intersections have an inside lane. If you don't know where you're heading, you can circle around until you either make your best guess or run out of gas. This, I presume, is why most island vacationers rent a Daihatsu.

Part of my problem was that I was using the rental car

agency's map. There's a pretty ingenious reason why these freebies are so impossible to decipher. As long as you can't find your way back to the rental return area, you have to keep paying for the use of the car.

Supposedly, my hands are to blame for my poor map reading skills. My index digits are longer than my ring fingers. This, according to a study conducted by German scientists, indicates that I'm less proficient at tasks requiring spatial skills than those who possess the more masculine finger length pattern (ring finger longer than index finger). Testosterone levels are thought to be responsible for this—as well as for most everything else that's researched primarily by men.

So guys, it appears that you can have either a gal who reads maps well or a lady without a mustache. But you can't have both. Don't argue with me about this because I'm not a German scientist. Quite possibly it's your fault that we've evolved this way. You see, women wouldn't need such long index fingers if men didn't always rely on us to point them in the right direction.

Vacation Envy

Right now, I'm dreading something more painful than summer gasoline prices, airport parking rates, or accidents with self-tanners. I'm anxious about receiving another trip itinerary from my dad.

You might say that my father is somewhat of an explorer, a guy who prefers venturing thousands of miles—he takes pride in logging and precisely reporting the exact number—in extreme heat to sitting comfortably at home with his remote. A devoted historian, he enjoys visiting distant locales and indigenous peoples—especially when he can reach these points of interest by cruise ship. The problem is this: When he sails, he thinks I should know the precise details of every leg of his excursion. Thus, he creates itineraries that I anticipate with a level of excitement normally reserved for holiday newsletters—which is to say zero.

Before his three-week tour of Australia and New Zealand, Dad typed out a schedule that not only included his flight and cruise departure times but also listed ports-o-call information. None of this seemed relevant to me because I wasn't going to be there.

At the bottom of a page, following 30 explicit line items

that all but revealed the longitude and latitude of Dad's whereabouts by the hour, as well as in which direction he'd be moving and what color attire he'd be wearing, he had finally listed the cruise operator's phone number.

Noticing this document magnetically anchored to my refrigerator, my daughter asked, "Why does he do this? He even tells you which days he'll be at sea."

Perhaps my father fears I suffer separation anxiety when he's gone, and he's trying to help me feel connected. However, I've way too many other mental challenges to adopt that one. To be honest, I think this is just Dad's way of saying, "Neh, neh, neh-neh, neh. I'm here and you're not."

If it is, then I have only this to reply: "Nener, nener, ne-ner. The norovirus won't get me."

My husband, Jim, and I share a lot of laughs and forehead slapping moments over my father's travel schedules, especially when we're discussing his method of delivery. Dad types his trip information on his computer, prints the pages, stuffs his itinerary into an envelope, affixes it with a stamp and mails it to me. And given my postal service, there's a chance that I might not receive his letter before he's returned home.

This year, Jim and I have decided to reverse this tradition. We're planning to deliver a vacation itinerary to Dad, one that reads something like this:

Day One

9:54-10:00 a.m.	Jim loads car
10:05-10:40 a.m.	Diana unpacks and rearranges luggage
10:45 a.m.	Vehicle departs driveway
10:50 a.m.	Return home to retrieve forgotten items
12:30 p.m.	Arrive at first McDonald's we see

12:45 p.m.	Depart McDonald's
3:35 p.m.	Arrive in Austin, stop for gas (both kinds)
3:40 p.m.	Depart Austin
4:30 p.m.	Detour to Gruene (home of state's oldest dance hall)
6:00 p.m.	Depart Gruene Dance Hall, arguing over who drives
6:45 p.m.	Arrive in San Antonio, The Coupon Hotel, 555-526-1674, Room # TBA
7:30-10:00 p.m.	Dinner and drinks on the Riverwalk
10:30 p.m.	Rescue Jim from river
11:00 p.m.	Return to hotel

On second thought, we better not follow through with this idea. I don't want to encourage Dad to become any more thorough than he already is. And I wouldn't want to make him feel jealous.

In case you're wondering, there's no need to fear that Dad will see this story because I've no intention of mailing it to him.

Bonaire or Bust

I won't ever reach the summit of Mount Everest or win the Tour de France. But those feats pale by comparison to flying on a Monday morning when certain airline employees just so happen to be engaged in salary negotiations.

It was a fair weather day that otherwise couldn't have been more perfect for air travel. All I desired was transport to the island of Bonaire, a destination I'd long dreamed of visiting, undoubtedly due to an overexposure to leisure magazines. But American Airlines must have divined that what I really wanted was to jog between Dallas-Fort Worth Airport terminals A and C—if these two points were any farther apart they'd be in different time zones—pulling my luggage as if I were a husky competing in the Iditarod, and then to take a detour to Miami. I was given the opportunity to equally test my endurance when the airline cancelled my flight from Miami to San Juan.

So after having two flights cancelled for "maintenance" issues, which I suspect is industry code for "unexplained employee absences," my spouse and I were stranded in Puerto Rico for 24 hours. Thus, we became guests of the Hump-N-Dump Hotel (name changed to protect myself).

Aside from the unwanted sex education I received through

the parchment thin walls at Hospitality Hell, I gained nothing from this mishap. Normally, I attempt to find the silver lining in these kinds of experiences. However, my intestines react differently, typically forcing me to look for the nearest restroom instead.

"You'll need to go to special services, at Gate 12," a harried flight attendant announced. "They'll give you a hotel voucher and work out the details." We'd arrived in San Juan too late to catch the one and only daily flight from there to Bonaire.

The tell-tale internal rumblings had begun. On top of this, I felt nauseous from lack of sleep and a landing that provoked me to silently chant, "We're all going to DIE!"

I prayed there'd be a lavatory somewhere between our arrival gate and Gate 12, or else we'd get to test just how "special" American Airlines' services could be.

We'd been up since 4:15 a.m. It was now after 7:00 p.m., and I was operating on airport vendor pizza and a toddler-size package of complimentary chips. My IBS (irritable bowel syndrome, aka "infinite bouts of shoo-shoo") was more aggravated than Al Gore after he learned of John Edwards' dependency on aerosol hairspray.

I dug inside my travel tote hoping to find anything that might stop the pressing "urge to purge."

Yes! There was something: a lone foil packet containing fragments of a broken pill. At a glance I could see the word "anti-diarrhea" printed on the back and the expiration date, "02/05," indicating it should have been tossed out a year earlier. I peeled off the aluminum and licked at the outdated medicine as though it might have been a fine Swiss truffle.

By the time we'd registered at the hotel, I'd developed a new facial tick and my body had begun producing whale noises. All I wanted was to sleep. Unfortunately, the all-night party in the adjoining room had just begun.

I won't bother to describe the sounds that filtered through my brief stints of slumber. But suffice it to say that I wasn't amused when, upon waking the following morning, my spouse feigned a wounded look and asked, "How come you never bark for me like that?"

"You can't pay me enough," I replied, which is pretty much how I feel about flying again, anytime soon.

DEEDEE'S BIG BONAIRE ADVENTURE

He tightened the adjustable strap on his ball cap. "Maybe I need a bandana instead of this hat," Jim said.

We were on the island of Bonaire vacationing, which is to say that we were ripe for doing something stupid.

Earlier that morning, when Mr. Explorer and I had checked at our resort's "activity center" (the place to enlist in ways to harm ourselves), we'd been told there were no available rental cars. If we wanted to see the entire island, we'd have to choose another means of transportation. Our choices were one motor scooter, two mopeds, or four feet. Given my aversion to exercise and inability to follow, we'd opted for the scooter.

Perhaps I should have foreseen the risks associated with riding on a motorized bike driven by a guy who has trouble recalling which handgrip is the brake. I hadn't thought much about the difficulties of trying to balance two bodies on one wobbly set of wheels or the 35 mph headwinds we'd encounter once we left the leeward side of the island. Nobody told us that the road narrowed to only a single lane near the South Point. And I'd not considered that all the directional signs would be written (or drawn) in Dutch. (For future reference, should you ever need to know, a triangular sign displaying red zigzag lines warns "dangerous curves ahead.")

In my mind I reasoned, "How hard can it be to ride a scooter? For goodness sakes, even Pee-wee Herman can do it."

"All ri-i-i-ight," said my mate, striking a mean pose atop our two-wheeler. "Get on, baby! You can be my motorcycle mama."

My bad boy was no Peter Fonda. More like *Easy Glider* maybe. But I didn't want to ruin his fantasies, so I climbed on and we took off.

What I didn't know was that Jim had never before driven a motor scooter, which meant that every time he needed to stop he decelerated and stuck out both feet. That worked okay until we met an oncoming truck—on a one-lane patch of roadway. This event gave me an opportunity to use the horseback-riding tricks I'd perfected in my youth. I now know that, when needed, I can still perform a rear dismount.

Once we had the pavement all to ourselves, I gained enough confidence to film our excursion. Ahead, in the distance, loomed pyramids of salt, their towering peaks glinting in the tropical light. We'd reached the salt flats that I'd read about, where mountains of brilliant white seasoning awaited ships' transport, a spot that contained enough sodium to bloat Calista Flockhart. Leaning, I fished through one pocket of my cargo pants to find my video camera.

My steady guide shouted, "What the heck are you doing back there? I'm about to run this thing off onto the shoulder!"

I knew he was lying because there was no shoulder. To our right, a rocky shoreline sloped off to a surging ocean. Flanking our left were rows of cactus.

"Let's head back to the other end of the island and get out of this wind," my navigator suggested.

"OK, but first, pull over here." I indicated a sign that pointed toward a beach road. Right then I had to get off that scooter and rest my glutes. For the first time ever, I wished I'd married someone 50 pounds thinner. Seated behind my partner, with my loins stretched and molded to his posterior, I felt like I was thigh-clutching a Clydesdale.

We coasted into the beach bar parking lot with Jim's legs jutting out like wings on either side of what I've nicknamed "the tourist eliminator." From inside an open-air café I could see the seashore, the windsurfers, and the ... What? Wait a minute. I thought topless sunbathing wasn't allowed in Bonaire!

"Didn't you see the sign when we pulled in?" My newly observant chauffeur chuckled. "It said 'naturalist beach.'" No wonder he hadn't objected to the detour.

Somehow, my weary limbs managed to make a full recovery after just one mango margarita.

Setting off for the north side of the island, the mountainous end, we snaked our way through a town and a group of free-range goats that had bolted across the street in front of us. I prepared to make another backwards escape, though thankfully one wasn't necessary.

Laden with both our weights, traveling uphill, the scooter couldn't go more than 15 kilometers per hour. Converted to miles, that roughly equates to a death crawl. A car full of locals zoomed up behind and then darted around us, passing so close that I lost a full day's growth of leg stubble. I glanced to see whether my left calf was still attached to me.

"I want off of here," I screamed. "Right now!"

Jim pulled to the side of the road and calmly offered, "I

better check and see how much gas we've got."

"What does the gauge show?" I huffed.

"It shows empty, but the rental lady told me the gauge was broken."

"Broken? How can we know if we have enough gas to get back?"

"She said to just open the tank and look."

He twisted off the lid and we both peered inside the dark cylinder.

We'd used up more than half our fuel supply. For the past hour we'd been meandering through the undeveloped end of the island, where a majority of the residents were iguanas.

The midday sun broiled our shoulders as we gingerly retraced our earlier route back towards town. Around every curve another car or truck driver seemed intent on taking us out. My legs cramped, neck burned, and stomach knotted. Any second now, my IBD (irritable bowel syndrome) was going to kick in. I wondered what it would be like to use cactus for toilet paper. "Please God, please, please, please, lead us to gas," I prayed. Suddenly aware that I should be specific, I added, "the kind that will get us back to the resort."

On fumes (both kinds) we drifted into a service station that we'd overlooked on our first pass through the village. Possibly the wandering livestock had distracted us.

"You'll have to get off of here," the Fearless One advised.

"Why?"

"Because, with you on back, I can't turn this thing tight enough to get to the pump."

I leapt from the scooter, performing another stellar rear dismount, thinking how fortunate I was. Not everyone has travel tales like this to share.

Scuba Lessons

Vacations scare me. Though I enjoy the rest and relaxation, problems occur when I try to chill out in foreign places, such as overseas, underwater, or around athletic people.

While in Bonaire, I was nearly killed by wild goats while riding on the back of a motor scooter. Apparently, charging at unsuspecting tourists is how these free-range animals beat island boredom.

On another trip, while snorkeling in search of the elusive manatee, I encountered the more prevalent Florida brown snake. The poisonous viper swam a serpentine path underneath my bare midriff. Hubby says he witnessed me exit the river while screaming and levitating inches above the water's surface. He claims it was a spiritual experience.

I should have anticipated there'd be trouble when I decided to obtain my scuba license. But my adventuresome spouse was working on his diver's certification, and I felt it was my duty to know how to rescue him.

On our first ocean dive, in Mexico, our boat captain remarked with confidence, "Don't worry. We only have to go out about a mile." What he didn't explain was that riding in a small dinghy on choppy seas turns passengers into human yo-yos.

By the time we arrived at the dive site, I felt dizzy and nauseous. I clung to the side of the boat like sea moss while my face turned a similar shade of lime green.

"Oh, I'm sick," I said.

Concerned, other divers immediately fell backward into the turquoise abyss.

"You'll be fine, once you get in the water," said the captain. "Just jump into the ocean."

My spouse gave me a reassuring look, and then, as any man confronted with similar circumstances might, he leapt over me and disappeared.

I sat alone on the wooden boat bench, bobbing up and down. Another half hour of this and someone would need to bury me at sea. Gingerly, I slipped into the waves, where I hoped to find relief—and my man—waiting.

Fifteen or so feet below me, I could just make out the blue stripe on my dive buddy's wetsuit. Descending, I swam to meet him.

Letting more air out of my BCD (buoyancy control device), I wondered if my natural "pontoons" would prevent me from sinking lower. It seemed that at any moment I might bob to the surface, rump first.

Eventually I reached the ocean floor where giant sea fans greeted me. The fragile coral undulated back and forth . . . back and forth . . . and back and forth. My stomach churned in counter time.

The air piping through my regulator tasted stale. I thought back to the most intriguing words my course instructor had said: "If you get sick, it's perfectly OK to vomit into your regulator."

In the deep blue surrounding me, way, way, way up overhead, I could see a small yellow circle. It turned out to be a Sergeant Major fish. But beyond that was a ring of light. And as my breakfast surfaced unexpectedly, I tried to do the same.

From out of nowhere, the dive master appeared. He grabbed me by my ankles and held tight. Shaking his head hard, he motioned to his dive computer. I could not safely ascend from this depth without pausing every 15 feet, for several seconds. Otherwise I'd get "the bends," a life-threatening medical condition that right then seemed preferable to what I was experiencing.

Chunks of food spewed through the appropriately named *purge* valves on either side of my regulator. This, in the underwater world, is the equivalent of shouting "free all-you-can-eat buffet!"

If there's anything more alarming than puking underwater, it's puking while aggressive fish and eels fight near your throat!

I'm not sure how much injury my fins caused the dive master, but I doubt that he needed to shave again for several weeks.

This year, I'm hoping for a safe vacation. All I want to do is go to the beach and snorkel without mishap. I have given up the scuba sport because I just don't have the stomach for it.

KEEPING THE HOLIDAYS "LITE"

Dopey Door Decorations

October is a spooky month because it calls into light some of the scariest people on the planet. Yep. Crafters.

Technically speaking, the fall equinox is responsible. This celestial event signals the official end of summer and spurs women into a frenzied quest for fake gourds and glue guns. Like geese heading south, ladies who've never once considered a subscription to Martha Stewart's *Living* migrate to their nearest hobby stores. There, these do-it-yourself designers purchase anything that resembles straw bales, ones that either have been or could be festively embellished. To better understand the seasonal search for straw, I decided, this year, to flank my fellow artisans of froufrou.

For my initial handicraft project, I chose an autumn wreath—that icon of suburban individualism that bears scant relationship to farmers, harvests, or pilgrims, yet it's intended to symbolize all three.

In case you'd like to join me and make your own door decoration, I'm providing these simple instructions. After each step outlined, I've included helpful remarks about my actual experiences during assembly.

Materials: 10-inch straw wreath purchased from craft store, items culled from your yard (leaves, nuts, acorns, etc.), a few dried sticks, ribbon, glue gun, spray acrylic, and newspaper

Instructions:

1. **In a well-ventilated room, spread newspaper to cover assembly area.** My breakfast nook opens to the kitchen and den, which I figured were ventilated enough, so I spread the newspaper over my dinette table.

2. **Place sticks on newspaper and spray with acrylic. Let dry, then spray again.** I couldn't find any twigs, so I substituted a few rawhide treats. (Note: Cinnamon sticks or leftover flautas might have worked equally as well.) The doggie chews already were shiny. However, I sprayed them with acrylic for good measure. After they'd dried, I shellacked them again, which caused me to giggle for no apparent reason.

3. **Hot-glue the sticks together and set aside.** My hot glue gun had stopped working, so I improvised. Who knew a curling iron could melt solid matter? (No wonder these devices can damage your hair!)

4. **Arrange items from yard on wreath and hot-glue into place.** Having searched my yard for intriguing items, I found only rabbit poo, a plastic Wal-Mart grocery sack, and my neighbor's dry cleaning receipt. So I painted the poo gold, cut and braided the bag, and crumpled the receipt into the shape of a maple leaf. One more shot of

metallic mist and a couple guffaws later, I could see my project beginning to unfold.

5. **Spray entire wreath with acrylic. Let dry.** Woo-hoo! Working with spray paints and acrylic is fun, let me tell you! You really can't use too much ac-- What's that stuff called, again? Oh, you know ... (tee-hee) too much of that shiny coating. My straw donut looked gorgeous, so while I was at it, I decided to color my nails. Ha! Ha! Ha! Look at me! I'm Goldfinger! Man, that aerosol varnish sure makes a good top coat!

6. **Spray wreath again with acrylic and let dry.** I am woman. I am Zen. I am one with the craftosphere.

7. **Tie ribbon around sticks and hot-glue them into place at the bottom center of wreath.** That pumpkin-print bow looked much prettier in my hair than it did on the wreath. I twined a couple of curly loops around my neck, and then, while I was searching for champaign glasses, the smoke alarms sounded. Right after that, a bunch of men in rubber boots and raincoats showed up at my front door.

Don't you just hate it when visitors arrive before you've even had a chance to hang your decorations?

Halloween "Hoochies"

You may never be too old to dress up for Halloween, but you could be beyond your prime for costumes such as Sea Goddess Mermaid. Think bare hips, exposed navel, and nearly nothing on top (the outfit, that is, not what's stuffed into it). The only person who wants to see me dressed like that is my gynecologist. And even he expects to be paid.

But for some women the desire to release their inner skank for fright night is stronger than a Miley Cyrus media hold. In fact, this trend is so universal that the Prostitute Pirate costume I found online is now available in ... wait for it ... plus sizes!

Regardless of age or heft, or for that matter even marital status, this time of year brings out the latent hoochie mamma in many. And retailers, aiming to please consumers, are happy to accommodate. That's why, when I go shopping for a party costume, I'm confronted with two basic choices: witch ensembles and "Whoa! I can't wear that!"

While lamenting the loss of my previous youthful figure, I confessed to a group of friends the difficulties of finding appropriate clothing. Another woman over 50 remarked, "Oh, I know! I mean, when I go out, I still want to look hot."

Hot? At my age, I'd be willing to settle for tepid!

But I've digressed.

Men, other than maybe ones like Richard Simmons, do not suffer these concerns. Guys don't select their Halloween costume or any other attire based on how much skin a getup permits them to display. No. That's unnecessary because they wisely intuit that, to appear irresistible to the opposite sex, all they have to do is equip themselves with either a tool belt, a vacuum cleaner, or a guitar.

However, we gals expect we need fishnet stockings to catch a man's attention. Either that or naked thighs, skimpy garb, and a humongous pair of earrings. You probably thought I was going to say something else, didn't you? I just didn't figure there was any point in mentioning that. Of course, everyone knows that what's most riveting to a guy is a 36-inch or greater size high definition TV.

This year, as usual, I've been invited to a Halloween party. But I'm leaving all the French maid outfits, naughty nurses' uniforms, and Elvira vampire dresses to the younger gals. They can traipse around in those revealing costumes all they want. I'll still be receiving plenty of attention because I know how to deal with that kind of competition.

I'm planning to layer on the self-tanners, throw on a blond wig and designer knockoff dress, and wear all my jewelry at once—including my best cubic zirconias! Yep, I'm attending the party disguised as a middle-aged heiress, one who might be looking for a new pool boy, another dependent—or possibly a place to park some venture capital.

So go ahead and show off all the stuff you want, girls. I've got enough years on you to know what best attracts male attention!

Skating with a Star

The holiday season can inspire people who would otherwise skip work because of a heavy frost to suddenly take their chances ice skating. Perhaps this is a result of exposure to Norman Rockwell. At least, that was my excuse.

I'd recently met a new love interest named Jim, and he'd asked if I'd like to go ice skating at a local mall. The annual Christmas tree had just been installed there, and, since shopping isn't something a man naturally thinks of when it comes to dating pursuits, he'd decided this might be the best way to connect with the festive atmosphere. Seemingly as an afterthought, he inquired, "Can you skate?"

"Uh, yeah, I think so," I stammered. "But it's been a while."

My response wasn't a lie. Jim hadn't asked if I could *ice* skate. In elementary school, I'd roller skated a few times.

"Great!" he said. "We'll go on Saturday."

As the weekend drew near, I discussed my concerns with a friend.

"Don't worry," advised my confidant. "As long as he can skate, he'll keep you vertical."

I'd never thought to check.

When we next spoke by phone, I pressed Jim about his

skill level and past experiences. And eventually I also worked my way around to asking if he could skate.

He quickly dismissed my fears. "I'm from Cleveland," he stressed, as though this automatically qualified him for the Winter Olympics. "And my ex-wife took figure skating lessons," he added.

Great," I thought. "I'm about to take my virgin pass around an ice rink with a figure skater's former partner.

When I laced up on Saturday, I felt the urge to confess. "You know, I've only roller skated in the past. This will be my first time on ice."

Jim helped me to my feet and gave my hands a loving squeeze. "It's going to be fun!" he enthused. With that air of confidence I admired in him, he guided me out onto the slippery floor. My legs buckled like a new filly's, but Jim held to me steadfast and soon we were off sailing ... OK, maybe not sailing, but shuffling along, hand in hand—just like Rockwell portrayed in his famous paintings.

Preschoolers buzzed around us like gnats, first gliding past us and then whipping around and skating backwards to taunt us with their superior command of gravity. Intimidated by these little showoffs, we picked up the pace.

Midway around the ice rink, I realized I didn't need to hover so close to the railing. Hurling my body across a frozen freeway was beginning to feel strangely normal, even thrilling.

"This is the way traditional holidays and love are supposed to be!" I'd no sooner thought this than one of those kindergartners shot past me, narrowly missing my free-floating toes.

Jerking one hand loose from Jim's grip, I lurched to prevent colliding with the wayward child. Then I made a dash for the side rail. Being the near-professional skater that Jim was, he surely would know how to correct for my unexpected move.

Behind me I heard jabs cutting through the ice. And when I looked over my shoulder, I saw what appeared to be a human tornado. In horror, I watched Jim perform asymmetrical (and clearly unintentional) rotations. Skaters parted to make way for the 160-pound man bent forward at the waist and spinning toward them with incredible inertia.

Jim's arms flailed in all directions as he fought, for what felt like eternity, to regain his balance. The violent swings of his appendages only served to accelerate his momentum. Silently I begged him to crash and get it over with. But he refused to give in.

This spiral of determination continued until my guy managed to slice and fling his way to the furthermost end of the rink, whereupon he at last clutched the guard rail and ground to a halt.

Overhead, from the mall level above us, a loud set of cheers and applause erupted. Throngs of teenagers showered Jim with their appreciation for his hilarious skating exhibition.

I'd done so well up to this point, but here's where that ended. I giggled until I expected this man would never speak to me again.

Jim, however, seemed impervious to embarrassment. Over a cup of hot chocolate, I later asked, "Why didn't you just let yourself fall? Didn't they teach you how to do that in those classes?"

He blinked. "I didn't say I took lessons. I said my ex did."

Obviously, we were a perfect match.

Seventeen years later, sometimes during the holiday season, one of us will fondly gaze at the other and ask, "Remember that time when we went ice skating?"

It's rewarding to have these kinds of Norman Rockwell memories.

What Your Gift Wrap Reveals

One of my biggest challenges during the holiday season is gift wrapping, which I try to do as little as possible. Any present that doesn't fit into a decorative bag ends up inside a trash sack tied off with a giant red bow.

My theory is this: A neat gift encased inside an unassuming package will favorably surprise whoever opens it, but a cheap present wrapped in expensive papers and ribbons fools no one. Those who attempt cleverness by disguising their gifts only succeed in divulging their social flaws.

And while I'm on that subject, if you want to know who in your family might be passive-aggressive, all you have to do is check the gift wrap. Packages secured with double-knotted ribbon or sealed with a half roll of tape (especially if it's duct tape) are dead giveaways. Also the narcissists can be easily identified. They're the ones who shout, "Open this one, first! It's from me-e-e."

Pathologically speaking, our clan fully illustrates the full range of the DSM-IV (a mental health diagnostic manual), minus a schizophrenic.

(What did you say? Oh, OK. The voices just told me I'm wrong about that. Apparently we have one of those, too.)

As I was saying before I was so rudely interrupted, camouflaging purchases unnecessarily creates hard feelings. Unless you're striving to alienate family members, it's best not to conceal your gifts in deceptively shaped or decorated packages. Don't stick that bird clock that someone gave you last year into fancy tissues and a sparkly gift bag and bestow it upon one of your guests. They'll simply think you're too lazy and pathetic to drive to the nearest Goodwill trailer.

If you're addicted to eBay and can't help bidding on other people's junk, then rent a storage unit, for goodness sake. Don't stuff that cybercrap into a pretty box and give it to someone who'll rightly want to injure you with it. That's no way to express your love or your concern for self-preservation.

One year, when I was a child, my father tried to fool my mother by exquisitely gift wrapping a case of Pepsi. Mom had been begging Dad for an electronic, portable organ she'd seen in Sears, and the box that contained this musical instrument was exactly the size of a case of bottled sodas. So Dad, in one of his many attempts to befuddle Mom, used creative wrapping skills no one knew he possessed to destroy all chances for a silent night.

As I recall, Mom eventually obtained the organ—and Dad narrowly escaped a concussion.

According to biblical scholars, the compulsion to use trickery when offering gifts dates back to three kings who, for obvious reasons, were known as the Wise Men. The first king is said to have presented the baby Jesus with a gift of gold. And then the next two, having let the first guy set the stage for future expectations, delivered frankincense and myrrh. Now, I can't say what was or wasn't appreciated about the items that essentially amounted to a bunch of tree sap, but I will point out that, in the Bible, there's no further mention of these three men.

Centuries later, another famous figure by the name of Santa Claus joined in the game when, instead of leaving toys, he surprised misbehaving children with lumps of coal. This, too, met with unforeseen consequences. It's rumored that, some years later, one of those grown kids founded a utility company. And we know who got the last laugh then!

Take a lesson from history and save your practical jokes for another occasion—unless, of course, a certain family member's condition might be improved by the sounds of cheerful chirping every half-hour. If you need a bird clock, I'll happily fork over the one somebody gave me last year.

A WORD ABOUT TOYS

There's no more enjoyable time of the year to be a parent or grandparent than at Christmas. As a grandmother, I get a hormone surge every time I see a Toys Я Us ad. My heart starts pounding, my pupils dilate, and I break out in a rash. And then I calm down when I realize that I've got a few good years left. My grandkids aren't yet old enough to ask for a PlayStation Roman numeral anything!

Isn't it wonderful when your children are in those early stages of life somewhere between "Where's Santa?" and "Who cares?" By the time they get to the 'tween age, holiday shopping loses some of its luster.

My grandchildren are ages 3 and 8, so I thought it would be easy to shop for them this year. Giddy with anticipation, I anxiously looked forward to shopping for teddy bears, Barbie dolls, Mumbles the dancing penguin, and Felony Elmo. (I say "felony" because you practically have to commit one to obtain him.)

I phoned my daughter-in-law, Julie, to see what the

children had been asking for.

"Oh, Heath wants something he can't have," said his mom.

"What is it?" I probed.

"A motorcycle," she said.

"Well, yes, I can see why you might not want to encourage him to bond with miniature models of dangerous transportation," I agreed.

"No. That's not the problem," Julie clarified. "The one he wants is real. It's at Wal-Mart, and it costs $199."

"OK, well then, what about Hannah?" I inquired, hoping to avoid any further hazardous requests. "Which Barbie does she want?"

"Actually, she's not asking for a Barbie, this year. She wants an electric scooter, an iPod, and an iDog."

I was not about to buy my granddaughter a guaranteed trip to an orthopedic surgeon. And after my husband screamed, "She's not getting an iPod before I even get one!" I realized that was out, too. So that left only the iDog.

It took two weeks for me to find this overrated, plastic, spastic mutt. The robotic beast lights up when he hears music. His head spins like the child's in a well-known horror flick, and his ears wiggle to the rhythm of whatever form of audio input has been provided. I've not actually seen one in action, but I gather this is how the contraption works.

Call me sentimental, but I miss shopping for toys that I can relate to—ones that remind me of my own childhood favorites. My playthings didn't sing and dance unprovoked, and nothing I possessed was powered by anything other than my two legs. Maybe that's why most of my generation remained physically fit in grade school.

Come to think of it, I've got the perfect gift ideas for my

grandchildren! I'm buying them a Big Wheel and a Pogo Stick.

GETTING THROUGH THE HOLIDAYS, DEEDEE STYLE

Deedee Divine's Helpful Holiday Tips

- Shop online–from inside your favorite coffeehouse or lounge.
- Decode product names. For example, an "i" at the beginning likely means "out of stock."
- Hide the remote ... and tell no one.
- Recognize that homicidal thoughts are normal, but please don't act on them.
- Pretend you're loaded–or just get that way.
- Don't revisit the past, even if you're invited.
- Multitask: let your grocer be your butcher, baker, and candy maker, too.
- Decorate by carefully arranging and spray painting past due notices.
- Store clutter in large boxes. Stack these cartons and cover them with a festive tablecloth to create extra seating.
- Put play money in your greeting cards.

- Gather up your board games and dispose of them before guests find them.

- Feng Shui your fridge.

- When possible, contract with professionals—especially if they're therapists.

THOUGHTS ON REGIFTING

I'm fairly certain that regifting originated from the need to dispose of a fruitcake. From there it branched out and became an ideal solution for eliminating all kinds of unwanted presents. Subsequently, entire industries have suffered.

As each new recipient acquired a regifted item, he or she then was able to eliminate one cheap and thoughtless purchase from a holiday shopping list. Think of it as multi-level sales in reverse. Manufacturers were forced to produce fewer goods, which in turn led to the nation's decline in GNP (Gross Needless Products). In fact, rumor has it that only one smoked sausage log has been made in the United States since 1978. Thus, regifting has become the bane of our economy.

If we'd all stop repetitively selecting the same purchases every year, then maybe we could put an end to this cycle of defeat. Just because every sales brochure we receive is hawking bathrobes at 50 percent off doesn't mean that anyone really needs one. Why do you think they're half-price and labeled "one size fits all"?

A terrycloth robe will be circulated through an entire extended family before someone donates it to the nearest homeless shelter. The same can be said for scarf and glove sets. Few Texas residents need a set of fleece-lined mitts. If you want to protect your loved ones here from harsh weather conditions, consider sending them lip balm and sunscreen.

This brings me to another ill-suited gift choice: throw blankets. I don't care if they are camo-print or have been made from those new super-soft petroleum-based fabrics. Grandpa doesn't sneak up on deer when he's sitting in his recliner. And polar fleece might very well be the single greatest factor contributing to global oil shortages. Besides, nothing says "You look like a person who has no social life" better than a blanket. This, too, is sure to be passed along until it's eventually claimed for dog bedding.

Speaking of possessions that guys don't actually use, here's another senseless acquisition—the auto emergency flashlight equipped with a ball peen hammer. Ladies, if the car breaks down, do you really want your man out there standing on the side of the road, fumbling in the dark, and trying to fix a vehicle with a demolition tool? And even if you are sadistic enough to answer yes to that question, that's not how these situations typically unfold. Most men would turn on the overhead dome light, flip open their cell phone, and dial AAA.

Women aren't the only ones who have difficulty making purchases for the opposite sex. Here's a tip for men who are shopping for their spouses: Ladies are not infatuated with sharp objects the way you are. Don't bother buying a knife set for your wife unless you mean to encourage sinister thoughts.

Furthermore, the cutlery industry has yet to recover from a butcher block steak knife set that someone purchased in 1982. This testosterone-laden object has since appeared at every bridal shower in the South. (Last seen, it was being offered on eBay by a seller whose name rhymes with "hobbit.")

Finally, let me offer a few words about loofah sponges: STOP GIVING THEM TO ME!

I'm sorry. I just had to get that out.

Similar to other females, I love smelling like freesia, though I'm not sure what that is. But I don't need a nylon scouring pad to apply my scented lotions and bath gels. These objects are fillers sold to the average consumer who believes there's a need for all this colorful netting. Apparently, this includes most anyone who's ever walked past the entrance of a Bath & Body Works.

While I can't get enough vanilla scented creams and soaps, I've had to dedicate an entire linen closet to the storage of unused loofah sponges. The problem here is that, despite regifting, I can't stay ahead of the influx of new arrivals.

Ultimately, regifting must be reduced to restore the financial health of our economy. The country's GNP depends upon all of us doing our part to make better informed purchases this season.

As to what to do with your unwanted bath aids, I can only suggest upgrading your home to one that includes more storage space. Nobody needs a loofah sponge. And our slumping real estate market could use the assistance.

Judging by the Light

As a newspaper columnist, I get asked to participate in all kinds of events. Some probably figure that if I've got the time to sit around and write this kind of drivel they should help me find a better use for my energies. Ha! They don't realize how difficult it is to sit here and poke fun at others who are doing something beneficial.

I accepted the prestigious honor of being one of three judges in a Christmas lighting contest. At first, I wondered how I had any credibility in the art of exterior illumination. And then I recalled my own outdoor decorations. Clearly, I'd displayed superior skills in the creative use of extension cord technology. That explained why I'd been selected. The fact that I was also the only one left in town who hadn't been invited to a posh party that night must have been a coincidence.

Since I didn't want to appear ignorant of lighting customs, I did some research before the contest. Did you know that in Victorian times people celebrated by lighting their Christmas trees with candles? No wonder so little of their residential architecture remains today!

The rage this year is a less flammable, self-inflating, outdoor decoration. I counted more than 25 of these giant balloons staked down in one subdivision. Inflatable snow globes imprisoning everyone from Santa to Winnie the Pooh glowed like UFOs that had mistakenly landed on lawns. King Kong-sized Disney characters peeked around house corners. One of these monsters appeared to be looking into a bedroom window, so he earned the title Voyeur Mickey.

It's amazing how many different tastes and styles are displayed this time of year. Holiday decorations often reflect more than colored light. They hint at the personalities of the corresponding residents.

I'd probably fit right in with the owners of the snowman holding a sign that reads, "All flakes welcome." Those are my kind of people.

Especially popular this season is something I call "the swag look." That's where a strand of lights has broken free and is now simply draping from one corner of a window or entryway. Quite contemporary. Maybe even a little avant-garde.

In one yard, all I could see was a lone, dead Santa. The fan required to inflate him had apparently been unplugged. Recognizing the address, I confirmed what my companions suspected. That home belonged to an accountant.

I love the houses where they've tried to cover all the bases: Santa Clause on the front porch, a manger scene occupying half of the yard, and a spattering of snowmen and penguins on the opposite side. You can bet the folks who live there are politically inclusive.

Some home dwellers must seek to confuse pilots. They're the ones whose linear driveways are bordered by a single row of red lights. These individuals appear to enjoy flirting with danger.

At the end of the evening after the neighborhoods had all been charted, viewed and scored, we had our winners.

"What happens if someone disagrees with our results?" I asked.

No one answered. Right then, it dawned on me that I was the only judge who had a mass-published e-mail address. And suddenly it was obvious why I'd been chosen for this job.

Self-inflatable Suckers

With SUV sales waning and gasoline users conserving, the petroleum industry has been forced to resort to holiday trickery. If you want proof of this, just drive around your neighborhood after dark and count the inflatable snowmen.

Perhaps you missed the connection between oil and gas and those 6- to 8-foot Frostys. At first, it escaped my attention, too. I was among the last to learn of the yard decorations that use what amounts to bouncy-house technology. Come to think of it, maybe the bouncy house is part of this conspiracy.

I first became suspicious when I learned of a utility company that had given away free Christmas lights to every household in Graettinger, Iowa, population 900. The power provider admitted taking this action to increase electricity demand.

"Ah-ha!" I cried during an Edison moment. "I bet those inflatables require heavy-duty, kilowatt-consuming fans." Sure enough, I confirmed this by checking several online sellers' sites.

These monstrosities stay inflated by burning electricity that's often generated by gas-powered utility plants. Furthermore, most of these air-filled displays are made of nylon. And nylon, as you may recall, is derived from petroleum.

Searching around, I found all kinds of inflatable

decorations, including a variety of 6-foot Disney characters and an 8-foot Homer Simpson. I even located a self-inflating, green Shrek that's dressed like Santa. What these cinematic symbols have to do with Christmas is beyond me, and I can't help wondering where we're going from here. The next thing you know, someone's yard display is going to include a set of blow-up dolls that look like the cast of *Desperate Housewives.*

The new trend is an inflatable snow globe that spews simulated precipitation, which is bound to use more energy than its predecessors. An ad for one of these behemoths suggests the ornament is suitable for both outdoor and indoor use. However, I don't know anyone who'd clear out their dining room to make way for one of these domes.

Perusing more advertisements for outdoor decorations, I laughed so hard I snorted when I read, "Super-size your Christmas ... inch by colorful inch." What, exactly, were they attempting to sell with that line?

An inflatable Christmas tree that's taller than me sells for less than $35. Why do you suppose it's so much cheaper than a real tree? Well, here's a hint: It wouldn't surprise me to find an Exxon label somewhere on that nylon noble fir.

Now, don't get me wrong. I'm not against outdoor decorations. What I'm saying here is this: Go ahead and park your car and turn down the thermostat. Those are good conservation measures to adopt. Just don't think that the oil and gas industry lacks a trump card. And if you should suffer an unexplained power loss this month, your neighborhood might want to consider pulling the plug on Frosty.

Silent Night (Hammer Sold Separately)

To the untrained ear, it probably sounded like an ordinary Burl Ives kind of day. A Christmas CD played softly in the background. Hunkered down in our favorite reading chairs, sipping on cups of hot chai tea and contemplating the arctic blast outdoors, my husband, Jim, and I practiced mirroring the relaxation techniques demonstrated by our cat. But soon this tranquil setting was interrupted by a foreign noise—and I don't mean Celine Dion.

"What's that sound?" I asked.

"Probably something you put in the dryer," said Jim.

"No. It was more of a scratching sound. Kind of like—"

"Wait," Jim interrupted. "I just heard it. It's coming from somewhere up there!" He pointed to an opening 9 feet above our den floor, a decorative space over our built-in entertainment center.

I gazed up to where he'd indicated. The artificial ivy I'd haphazardly stuffed inside a wicker basket and shoved into this remote cavity rustled. About that time our cat, who'd been doing her best throw pillow impersonation, came to life.

"A-a-a-a-ah! There it IS!" I screamed.

Peering down at me was a rodent of some sort. I studied its

size and then with relief announced, "It's just a little field mouse." Edging in closer, I climbed a chair to get a better look. The startled visitor froze in place as I pulled to eye level with him.

Jim jumped to his feet and, displaying his usual compassion, remarked, "Get me my hammer."

"What?" I cried. "Don't you dare! Why, he's nothing but a harmless Christmas mouse. He's Stuart Little, for goodness sake. Come look at this cute fuzzy face," I begged. "How could you even think of pounding this defenseless creature?"

"You're right," agreed my mate. "I'll run to the store and get some traps."

Upon hearing this, Stuart dashed into a crack that I wouldn't have known existed had I not been standing on a bar stool (for the first time, I might add, in years).

It seems that our homebuilder had left a half-inch gap between the cabinetry surface and the drywall. Apparently this mouse had mistaken the opening as an invitation to tour our home.

"You are not going to kill this poor thing," I declared. "I won't let you do it." I squared my shoulders and gave the mouse musher a stern look.

"Well, what, exactly, do you recommend?" he scoffed. "And before you say it, don't even tell me you want to keep it for a pet."

"Of course I don't want to keep it for a pet. I'm going to trap it and return it to the outdoors, where it belongs."

"Sure you are."

Mr. Know-it-all sneered before retreating to another room.

I fired up my laptop computer and typed in "no kill mouse traps," then hit the search button to see what might prevent Jim from any further urges to play whack-a-mouse.

Sure enough, I found several descriptions of how to design a homemade trap, accompanied by instructions on what to do with these interlopers once they've been caught.

"Take the mouse at least one mile away before setting it loose," several Web sites recommended. Like squirrels, field mice are so fiercely territorial that they have no problem duplicating *The Incredible Journey*. These creatures can, and do, return when they're released too near their home origin.

Carefully following the instructions, I creased a cardboard insert from a toilet paper roll (to make part of the tube flat) and set a Ritz cracker slathered with peanut butter inside one of the open ends. Next, I balanced the tunnel to freedom on the ledge above the entertainment center. The tube precariously teetered above a two-foot tall, galvanized aluminum florist's can. If all went as planned, the mouse would enter the chute, crawl out onto the opposite end to retrieve the cracker, and tip the cardboard cylinder. The victim would then perform a double-gainer into the canister, and if he was lucky, the treat would land shortly thereafter—peanut butter side up.

To insure that I could quickly retrieve the trap when it was triggered, I had positioned the flower bucket at the top of a stepladder. I expected to climb the ladder, throw a piece of aluminum foil over the container's opening, and dart for my car, carrying the soon-to-be-relocated rodent.

About an hour later, the intruder stuck out his head and sniffed.

Hallelujah! It was working.

The mouse skittered across the ledge, but instead of entering the tube from the backside, he nudged underneath the trap in an attempt to dislodge the treat while maintaining his current position.

Great. I had an intellectual on my hands.

With this unexpected turn of events, the trap and the cracker dropped into the flower can. Stuart, however, did not. Instead, he leaned perilously over the cabinetry and appeared to be calculating his chances for survival should he leap.

Stealthily I climbed the ladder, lifted the pale, and opened one of the uppermost cabinet doors beneath the ledge to get a better aim at this crafty fellow. I would lure him into the can, if possible.

The mouse charged at me, full speed, and leapt onto the cabinetry trim. Now he was 2 inches from me at chest level. I screamed and tried to reverse down the ladder but discovered that the cat had followed me up the steps. Our normally sedate kitty was perched directly below my feet and ready for action. She bleated predator-like warnings at the moving object. Any second now, she would likely use my backside to launch herself closer to the toy of her dreams.

Stuart made a break for the open cabinet where I stored all of my old LPs, the vinyl remnants of my youth, the last tangible evidence that, yes, indeed, I had once been cool. I slammed the door shut, trapping the unwanted houseguest, confining him to spend time with the likes of Super Tramp and The Little River Band.

About this time, Jim wandered in to see what all of the ruckus was about. "He's in there," I explained, pointing to the sealed door, "with the music of my past."

"You let him get in there!" he accused. "Why did you do that? How are you going to get him out, now?"

From the ladder I glared down at him. "Could you please just move this cat?"

"You know, I could fix this whole thing right now with my hammer," he reminded.

"Look, if you want to be helpful, why don't you just take

these albums as I hand them down to you? He's crawled behind them, somewhere."

Reluctantly, Jim agreed—probably so he could stand there and make fun of me.

It wasn't until I removed the final 10 or so records that the field mouse lunged forward again, threatening to scale my torso.

Jim grabbed the flower bucket and, showing utmost restraint, refrained from using it as a mallet. The mouse leapt into the can. Finally, I had this little gray guy in my custody.

"Quick," I yelled, taking possession of the prisoner. "Get some foil!"

After I'd secured the patty pot, I grabbed my car keys and a flashlight and sprinted to the garage. I was about a half mile down the road before I realized I was wearing only my house shoes and pajamas.

It was dark outside, and the temperatures were hovering somewhere in the low 20s. The florist's container stood in the passenger seat next to me, and every once in awhile I heard foil crinkle. Was my prisoner trying to make a break? What if he got loose inside my car? How would I find him? Better still, would my husband ever let me live this down? I could see myself serving tool duty for the rest of my life.

Outside the city limits near a bridge, I pulled to the shoulder of the road. Here were plenty of trees and brush and a water source. Why, Stuart could not only find a nice home, but he could practically start his own subdivision. I opened the driver's side door and retrieved the canister, noticing that it felt too light to be occupied. If there was a mouse in there, you'd have never known it.

My teeth chattered in the night air. I pulled my flannel top tight around my neck, attempting to block out the 25 mph wind gusts and feeling like an animal activist idiot. Placing the container on its side, I removed the foil covering. Nothing. Not a sound. I shined the flashlight in a circle. No movement of any kind. Directing the beam into the bucket, I found only empty space.

This was a freakish nightmare, worse than watching the movie *Ben*! While I was standing out here on a country road in the dark with no coat and on the verge of frostbite, Houdini the Vermin was inside my running vehicle, conducting magic tricks from my heated leather seats. His hairy butt was mine!

I had been having a perfectly normal, sedentary Sunday until this thumb-sized nuisance had reared his rat-looking head. All I'd ever wanted was for him to return to his rightful home and to vacate mine, but NO-O-O. He had to go and make matters difficult. He had to put up resistance. This is the thanks I get for trying to save his stupid, short life! In my head I heard the music of the Sixties—Peter, Paul, and Mary, to be exact. And I knew right then what I'd do if I had a hammer!

I lifted the flower bucket and thought how best to use it when I next found Stuart.

Right as the canister cleared the ground, leaves rustled. I trained my flashlight on the direction of the sound just in time to see a mouse scurry beneath some twigs.

Mission accomplished.

"Did you set him loose?" Jim asked when I returned home.

"Yep."

"You know, of course, that he's going to freeze tonight ... that is, unless something eats him first."

Later that evening, I heard a strange sound and decided not to search it out.

The following day, when I drove past the mouse release site, I noticed a sign that read, "Coming Soon! Estate size lots." I couldn't help but wonder how recently it had been erected.

A Personal Companion for Christmas

"Here's what you can get me for Christmas," Jim said, snapping his newspaper. "It says right here that some local guy is building personal robots that look like humans and can respond to any conversation." Mr. Wise Guy cut his eyes at me and chuckled.

"I'm still waiting to find a spouse that responds to any conversation," I fired back.

"Hey," said my fantasizing hubby, "just think. Your replacement could be voice-activated and designed to only give compliments!"

I considered this for a moment and then quipped, "You mean, like, 'No, your gut could never look big?'"

Jim shot me a look that said "touché" and then added, "Definitely, mine would have to come with a mute button."

While he sat there cracking himself up with his verbal game of one-upmanship, I marveled at the possibilities of obtaining a programmable partner.

"The price tag is a little steep," he continued, "but when you consider that a robot wears the same clothes every day ... I suppose $130,000 might be a bargain!" He kept yammering about how an android could be better than a wife, citing advantages like, "She'd never wrinkle or suffer PMS" and "She'd probably even perform her own car repairs and squish bugs."

His riff made me think about placing my own custom order for a computerized companion, one that wouldn't complain when asked to unstop toilets, clean exterior windows, or rotate my auto tires. This mechanical mate wouldn't need to be all that chatty. A few pre-recorded phrases would suffice: "Yes, Dear," "I'd be happy to do that for you," "You look *fabulous*," and "Would you like the remote?" would cover most of the bases.

As a special feature, I'd want my electronic slave to double as an ATM—which my current man claims he does now. The difference would be that the robot wouldn't ask me to explain why I needed the money. He'd never accusingly remark, "But you already have two pair of black shoes!"

I'm pretty sure there'd be downsides to having an artificial lover, though. In my earlier years, I dated a few. But I mean one with artificial, as opposed to insufficient, intelligence.

First, I'd have to trade in the fellow I tease, complain about, and skewer in my columns and books. Then, I'd wind up possessing the kind of guy that other women would want to steal, which is not to suggest that the one I have now isn't worth nabbing. It's just that, for any new owner, he'd be much more difficult to reprogram.

Finally, I'd lose my sympathy card, people would stop feeling sorry for me, they'd quit reading my work, and then I'd have to get a real job, the kind where you are forced to do painful things, like get dressed every day before the evening news airs.

So, for now, I think I'll forego this futuristic technology.

I don't want a new personal companion because, when it comes to robots, I'm attached to the one I already have.

During the holidays, it's easy to forget that the best gifts are often the ones we receive every day. Sure, my spouse might obtain better domestic service from Rosie Robot. However, his brain would shrivel to the size of a walnut from the lack of marital friction. And, you know, she'd never make Jim famous.

Acknowledgments

First, I'd like to thank everyone who bought, borrowed, or found this book through some other means and read all the way to this page. You deserve a reward! Please buy yourself something and pretend it's from me because I'm still paying off my debts from my last book tour.

I want to express my deepest gratitude to my husband, children, and parents who so generously (and often unwittingly) supplied much of my story material. Thank you for allowing me to exploit and exaggerate your endearing quirks without threat of lawsuit. This book would not have been possible without your love and support.

Another round of applause goes to my editor Matt Dewald, who worked tirelessly, through a hurricane and at times without electricity, to make me appear much smarter than I actually am.

I'm also indebted to Michelle Tedford for her patience, creative vision, and book design expertise. Without assistance from fellow humor author Tim Bete, I might never have found key team members Matt and Michelle. Thank you, Tim.

I'd like to recognize a few women who cut this trail before I did. The works of Erma Bombeck led me to the joys of humor writing, and Southern humorists Susan Reinhardt and Celia Rivenbark graciously provided further encouragement.

To all my pals who cheered me to the finish line, I am anchored by your kindness and friendship.

About the Author

Diana Estill's essays have been published in a variety of newspapers, magazines, journals, and books. Her opinion columns have appeared in *The Dallas Morning News* for more than a decade. She is the author of *Driving on the Wrong Side of the Road: Humorous Views on Love, Lust, & Lawn Care.*

Diana lives in Texas with her husband, Jim, who doesn't mind being a foil if it will one day make him famous.

Printed in the United States
218024BV00001B/17/P

9 780979 970818